MORE DEADLY THAN WAR

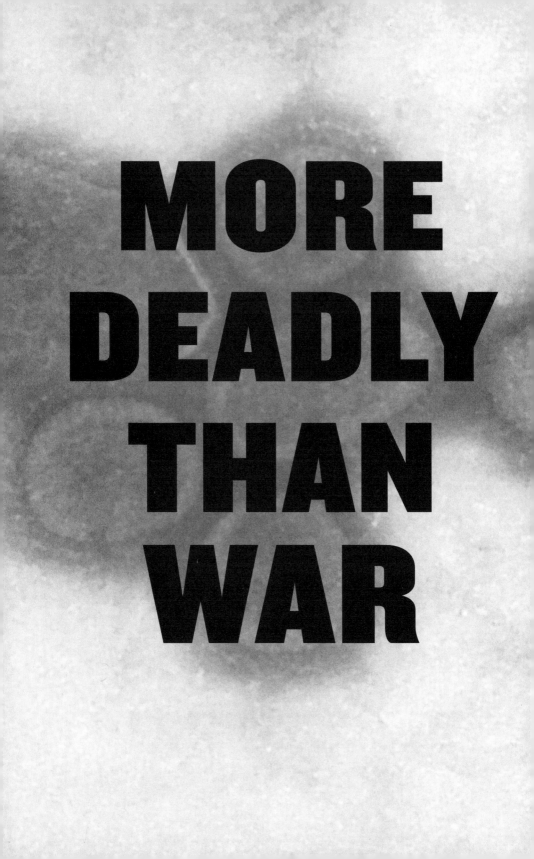

MORE DEADLY THAN WAR

THE
HIDDEN HISTORY
OF THE
SPANISH FLU
AND THE
FIRST WORLD WAR

KENNETH C. DAVIS

Henry Holt and Company

New York

Henry Holt and Company, *Publishers since 1866*
Henry Holt® is a registered trademark of Macmillan Publishing Group, LLC
120 Broadway, New York, NY 10271 • mackids.com

Image on pp. ii–iii courtesy Cynthia Goldstein Centers for Disease Control
and Prevention Public Health Image Library. Additional credits are noted
with captions.

Library of Congress Cataloging-in-Publication Data
Names: Davis, Kenneth C., author.
Title: More deadly than war : the hidden history of the Spanish flu and the
    First World War / Kenneth C. Davis.
Description: First edition. | New York : Henry Holt and Company, 2018 |
    Includes bibliographical references and index. | Audience: Ages 10-14.
Identifiers: LCCN 2017041236 | ISBN 9781250145123 (hardcover) |
    ISBN 9781250145130 (ebook)
Subjects: LCSH: Influenza Epidemic, 1918-1919 —Social aspects —Juvenile
    literature. | Influenza —Patients —Anecdotes —Juvenile literature. | World
    War, 1914-1918 —Juvenile literature.
Classification: LCC RC150.4 .D38 2018 | DDC 614.5/1809041 —dc23
LC record available at https://lccn.loc.gov/2017041236

Our books may be purchased in bulk for promotional, educational, or
business use. Please contact your local bookseller or the Macmillan
Corporate and Premium Sales Department at (800) 221-7945 ext. 5442
or by email at MacmillanSpecialMarkets@macmillan.com.

First edition, 2018 / Design by Christine Kettner
Printed in the United States of America by LSC Communications,
Harrisonburg, Virginia

10 9 8 7 6 5 4 3 2

DEDICATED TO THE BRAVE "SALLIES"
OF THE SALVATION ARMY,
THE RED CROSS "ANGELS,"
AND ALL THE OTHER NURSES WHO WENT TO
THE TRENCHES AND SICK WARDS IN 1918—
AND TO ALL THOSE NURSES WHO CONTINUE
THE NOBLE TRADITION OF THEIR PROFESSION

CONTENTS

African American troops were among the first U.S. troops dispatched to France. *[Library of Congress]*

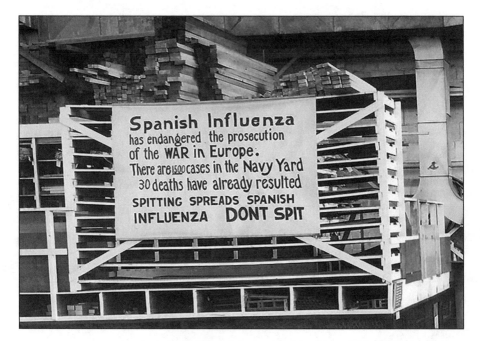

A sign posted at the Philadelphia Navy Yards in 1918 made it
clear: the Spanish flu and what came to be called
World War I were inseparable. *[U.S. Naval Historical Center]*

What's true of all the evils in the world is true of plague as well. It helps men to rise above themselves.

—*Albert Camus*, The Plague *(1947)*

MORE DEADLY THAN WAR

INTRODUCTION

THE PURPLE

I had a little bird,
Its name was Enza,
I opened up the window,
And in flew Enza.
—Children's jump rope song, 1918

DEATH

IT WAS 1918 in the Alaskan outback, far from the muddy, bloody trenches of the Great War raging across Europe. The town of Brevig Mission, on the remote Seward Peninsula, was about as far as you could travel at the time and still be in American territory. (Alaska was not yet a state.) The people of Brevig Mission didn't have to worry about the tanks, bombs, airplanes, and mustard gas that were wreaking havoc in France and

Belgium. The dangers of a world war meant little in this small fishing village near the Arctic Circle.

Then the native villagers were hit by a strange malady. It began simply enough with coughs and sore throats, followed by extremely high fevers. The villagers complained of severe headaches, pain behind their eyes, and excruciating muscle aches. Keeping food down was impossible—men, women, and children were vomiting uncontrollably. Soon the people of Brevig Mission were coughing blood and choking on their own mucus.

Five days later, seventy-two of the village's eighty inhabitants were dead. Rescuers who eventually reached the Lutheran mission there found little more than bones and corpses, which had been ripped apart by starving dogs. In one igloo, they discovered three children huddled together in the midst of their dead family. Living on oatmeal, they had miraculously survived several days in the unheated ice hut.

The dead were buried in a mass grave dug from the frozen earth, or permafrost.

Elsewhere in Alaska, in places that could be reached only by boat or mushers in dogsleds, other rescue teams found many more horrific scenes. In the small fishing outpost of

PREVIOUS PAGES: Children left orphaned by the Spanish flu in Nushagak, a remote village in the territory of Alaska, where the pandemic devastated the native population in 1918 and early 1919.
[Alaska State Library]

Crosses mark a mass grave of Spanish flu victims at Brevig Mission in Alaska. *[Ned Rozell, National Library of Medicine, National Institutes of Health]*

Micknick, a Red Cross medical team found thirty-eight adults and twelve children dead. Across the Naknek River, the team reached another village with a seafood cannery. In the "barabaras"—traditional Aleutian sod houses that are partially underground—they found twenty-two of the twenty-four adults there had died; a twenty-third death followed the next day. Many of the victims had bluish skin, the reason some people called the mysterious sickness the Purple Death.

"Numerous villages were found but no sign of life about," the Red Cross team reported, "except for packs of half-starved, semi-wild dogs." The report continued, "It was impossible to estimate the number of dead as the starving dogs had dug their way into many huts and devoured the dead, a few bones and clothing left to tell the story."

The Purple Death was actually part of a great wave of influenza, a lethal virus that swept across America and around the world starting in the spring of 1918. A second, even deadlier wave of influenza appeared in late summer and autumn of 1918, and a third wave continued into 1919. This highly contagious disease, later widely known as Spanish flu, killed an estimated 675,000 Americans in one year, according to historian and professor Alfred Crosby.

Consider this perspective: more Americans died from the flu in this short time than all the U.S. soldiers who died fighting in World War I, World War II, the Korean War, and the

A native Alaskan barabara, or sod house. *[Gulf of Maine Cod Project, NOAA National Marine Sanctuaries; courtesy of National Archives]*

Vietnam War combined. Indeed, the Spanish flu killed as many Americans in about a year as did HIV/AIDS, the most notorious epidemic of modern times, in more than thirty years. According to the Centers for Disease Control and Prevention (CDC), the estimated number of deaths from diagnosed HIV infection classified as AIDS in the United States since the first reported death in 1981 through 2014 was 678,509—about the same number that died of Spanish flu from 1918 to 1919.

And America was not suffering alone. This was not an

Alaskan natives contracted and died from influenza in disproportionately high numbers. *[Library of Congress]*

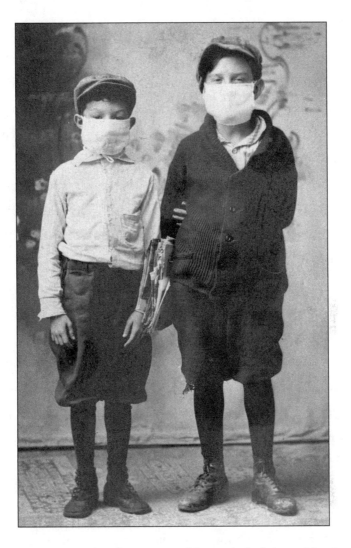

Two boys wearing masks, the most visible symbol of the epidemic as it swept the world in 1918. *[Florida State Archives]*

epidemic but a pandemic—a widespread outbreak of a killer disease—that eventually swept over the whole world. From the spring of 1918 and on through the winter of 1919–20, waves of influenza deluged the world like a global tsunami.

Rearing its head first in America, it has long been thought, Spanish flu spread its devastation across Europe and into Africa, India, New Zealand, and the Philippines. It knew no borders or boundaries. It struck kings, presidents, and generals, average soldiers and civilians, rich and poor alike. It killed Germans and Americans, Alaskans and Africans. Never before—or since—had an outbreak of the flu been so murderous.

For many years, the Spanish flu pandemic's death toll was estimated at twenty to fifty million people around the world. That would make it the second most lethal pandemic in world history after the notorious Black Death, a series of catastrophic plagues that engulfed Europe, Asia, and the Islamic world in the 1300s. The Black Death killed an estimated seventy-five million people, with the real possibility that as many as two hundred million people died.

Recently, medical researchers have come to believe that the death toll from the Spanish flu of 1918–19 was much greater than first thought. India alone lost 18.5 to 20 million people. According to revised estimates, scientists now suggest that the worldwide tally from the Spanish flu may have reached 100 million dead—a figure that would have been about one person in twenty alive in 1918, or around 5 percent of the world population. Many more people were sickened by the flu, with long-lasting effects.

We live in a world in which we fear the deadly things we can see. Bombs, guns, and terrorism are the most visible threats to life and peace. History books are filled with accounts of wars that have killed millions of people.

But throughout human history, the things we cannot see have actually been the most lethal. Diseases have been more deadly than war. While many schoolbooks and historians tend to focus on great battles and the military decisions of kings and generals, history's greatest killers have been the tiniest foes—microscopic parasites, bacteria, and viruses that have wreaked havoc on civilization. Only in fairly modern times has science been able to see these minute killers, understand how they function, and learn how to fight them.

There is no better example of this fact than what took place in 1918, as the world suffered through the global conflict now called World War I. Known then as the Great War, and optimistically called "the war to end all wars," World War I ultimately took the lives of an estimated fifteen to twenty million people—soldiers and civilians. The unprecedented carnage of twentieth-century mechanized warfare shocked the world.

"Children lost fathers, wives husbands, young women the chance of marriage," writes historian Margaret MacMillan. "And Europe lost those who might have been its scientists, its poets and its leaders. And the children who might have been born to them. But the tally of deaths does not include those who were left with one leg, one arm or one eye, or those whose lungs had been scarred by poison gas or whose nerves never recovered."

Coming amid these unthinkable wartime casualties, the Spanish flu dwarfed World War I's staggering human toll. The Spanish flu's murderous reign was more terrible than the bullets and bombs, and wartime conditions only made matters worse. Refugees crowding cities, malnutrition, and shortages of doctors, nurses, and effective medications all contributed to the pandemic's rapid spread and high rates of death. But it was the movement of troops—with men crowded together in barracks, tents, and trenches and jammed onto railroad trains and ocean-going troop transports—that was most responsible for the spread of the Spanish flu.

The outbreak of the Spanish flu in the spring of 1918 coincided with the last months of fighting in World War I, which ended on November 11, 1918. Through documents and the voices of the people who experienced these twin catastrophes, this book tells the story of a devastating disease and the people it affected. It tells how entire armies, great cities, and small towns were overwhelmed by death. It is a tale of families broken and destroyed, of lives shattered. It is a tale of heroism by the medical professionals and volunteers who desperately attempted, yet largely failed, to contain the disaster. And it is a scientific mystery of a virus that eluded detection—a puzzle solved only recently.

GIVEN THESE HORRORS, it is somewhat surprising that the devastation caused by the Spanish flu has been hidden in history books. Many accounts of World War I detail army tactics and political maneuvers but barely mention the Spanish flu. Some overlook it entirely. "The flu was expunged from newspapers, magazines, textbooks," science writer Gina Kolata states, a form of "collective amnesia."

"The average college graduate born since 1918 literally knows more about the Black Death of the fourteenth century than the World War I pandemic," writes historian Alfred Crosby. He suggests that when combined with the catastrophic losses of World War I, the period was so dreadful that people simply did not want to think or write about it. It fell into a black hole of history.

The origin of the pandemic's name was itself an odd result of the war. This particularly deadly burst of "Spanish influenza" did not come from Spain. When the epidemic first struck, most of the warring countries restricted what newspapers could print. They didn't want their enemies to know that they were weakened by the flu. And they hoped to keep morale high in their countries.

A neutral nation during the war, Spain did not censor its newspapers, which published reports of the epidemic. By the time Spanish authorities realized that the nation's reputation was being damaged, it was too late. The name stuck.

Soon known in many places as Spanish flu— or the Spanish Lady—the disease went by many other names as each country tried to point a finger of blame. In Spain it had been christened the Naples Soldier, the name of a popular Spanish song of the day. Germans called it the Russian Pest. The Russians called it the Chinese flu. In Japan, it was wrestler's fever. In South Africa, it was known as either the white man's sickness or *kaffersiekte*, blacks' disease. Soldiers fighting in the Great War called it the three-day fever—a highly inaccurate description—and when it first struck in the spring of 1918, German soldiers called it Flanders fever, after one of the war's most notorious and deadly battlefields.

Whatever name it went by, the reality of the Spanish flu was horrible. As it hurtled around the world in 1918, panic set in when some people

Several cities began to require the use of gauze masks.
Although many people dutifully wore masks, they provided
limited protection against the influenza virus.
[Office of the Public Health Service Historian]

dropped dead on the streets. Victims with high fevers, unbearable headaches, and severe coughing that brought up blood inundated hospitals. Stacks of decomposing bodies overwhelmed city morgues. There were shortages of coffins, and funeral parlors could not keep pace with the demands of grieving families.

Desperate but mystified doctors and public health officials tried anything. Many recommended wearing a gauze mask, similar to a surgical mask. In some places, these masks were even required by law. In San Francisco "mask slackers"—people not wearing masks—were subject to fines or jail.

Caused by a virus, the Spanish flu hit at a time when science did not fully understand what a virus was. Coined in 1892, the term "virus" refers to things much smaller than bacteria, which had been seen in early types of microscopes. Before 1930, microscopes were not yet powerful enough to reveal the viruses that cause the flu and other diseases, so these infinitesimal particles had never been seen. Many scientists of the day mistakenly believed that some type of bacteria caused influenza, commonly called the flu today.

The word "influenza" was first used in English in 1743 and is thought to come from an eighteenth-century Italian phrase *influenza di freddo*, which means "influence of the cold." The Italian phrase may have come from the earlier Latin *influentia coeli*, or "heavenly influence," a reference to the idea that

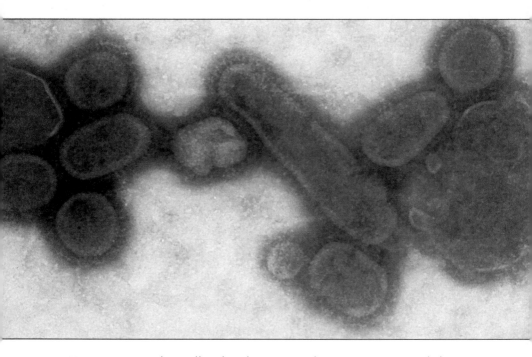

Viruses are much smaller than bacteria and were not seen until the development of the electron microscope in the 1930s. *[Cynthia Goldstein Centers for Disease Control and Prevention Public Health Image Library]*

illness and disease came from astrological influences—the stars in the sky.

In ancient Greece, the physician Hippocrates, considered the father of Western medicine, cataloged flu symptoms more than 2,400 years ago. He described headache, fever, body aches, and severe coughing, which typically appeared in early winter and ended by springtime—what is now commonly known as flu season. Over the centuries, influenza also went by such names as the grippe, catarrh, and the sweating sickness.

When the Spanish flu struck the world in 1918, accurate information was scarce, mass media was limited, and government officials sometimes deliberately withheld information, using censorship to avoid panic and maintain public morale.

This is the story of how the world tried to cope with a disaster whose global reach was unprecedented in modern times. It is a story of people desperately battling an illness that seemed like no other. It is the story of science's distressed dash to find answers to a medical mystery.

It is also a story of how propaganda was used to shape public opinion. When the war broke out in 1914, newspaper accounts and government reports of atrocities made people fear other nations by calling them "barbaric." When the flu hit in 1918, the public feared a disease they did not understand, and many were told that the enemy had spread the disease. Today, when propaganda and other types of "fake news" are filling the media and Internet, it is important to understand and recognize facts—about history, politics, religion, and disease.

The Spanish flu spread so quickly and so far because the world was going through a form of globalization—trade and travel on a widespread, international scale. In this case, that travel was brought about by war. During the Great War, people in very large numbers traversed the globe on ships and trains. Now people who might carry infectious diseases are also able to move around the world on jets and high-speed trains. In an era of global commerce, deadly diseases can be carried on large container ships that link the continents. The world has grown much smaller. Ignorance, poverty, conflict, natural disasters, and climate change still create the breeding grounds for terrible epidemics.

Since 1918, science has learned much about influenza and other serious illnesses. Once fatal on a wide scale, such mass killers as polio, malaria, and smallpox have largely been eradicated or brought under control. Of course, there are many things science does not yet understand or can't fully explain. New threats emerge constantly, and such headline-making outbreaks as AIDS, Ebola, Zika, and new strains of flu can pose serious worldwide health dangers. But facing questions with sound reason and clear thinking usually produces much better decisions and results than blindly allowing unjustified fear and uninformed opinion to take over.

We can learn from the story of the Spanish flu. It is about how real people lived through one of the world's greatest calamities, and how many of them responded with courage and self-sacrifice. It is about how the disease came to pass, and what we should all know about the dangers that still exist in our increasingly globalized world. Only by uncovering this piece of the past can we make use of its lessons today.

CHAPTER ONE

"THE YANKS

ARE COMING"

I gather that the epidemic of grippe which hit us rather hard in Flanders also hit the Boche [Germans] rather worse, and this may have caused the delay.
—Harvey Cushing, American army surgeon, June 1918

R USSELL AND WALT were itching to fight. It was the summer of 1918, and for two sixteen-year-olds, getting into a uniform was all that mattered. The whole country was seized by war fever. Young men across America flocked to sign up.

A year after America had finally entered the Great War, a patriotic frenzy filled the air. Posters plastered around the country showed Uncle Sam declaring, "I Want You." Everyone was singing "The Yanks are coming"—the words to the hit tune "Over There" by America's most popular song-and-dance man, George M. Cohan. American soldiers had proudly

James Montgomery Flagg's recruiting poster became
the most famous image of Uncle Sam.
[Library of Congress]

In America, government posters depicted the Germans as ruthless killers who fought without regard for civilians. *[Library of Congress]*

marched into Paris. The navy promised adventure and a chance to beat back the Germans—who were disparaged as barbaric "Huns" in the American press and government posters.

Walt's older brother, Ray, had been drafted into the army

Navy recruiting poster from 1918.

and wrote how exciting life was in training camp. Another brother, Roy, had enlisted in the navy and was stationed at the Great Lakes Naval Station near Chicago.

Like many young Americans, Walt saw going to war as a great quest—the stuff of heroes. He was fired up to do his part to defeat the dreaded Huns. He wasn't a slacker. Walt yearned to be "over there" in full army gear. Like many young Americans, Walt thought he would look "swell" in a uniform.

Russell and Walt lied about their ages, but the recruiters in their home city of Chicago took one look at the pair and sent them home disappointed. Then Russell learned that the American Red Cross Ambulance Service accepted seventeen-year-olds. Their job was to collect wounded men from the battlefield. Another teenager from nearby Oak Park, Illinois, eighteen-year-old Ernest Hemingway, had joined the ambulance service in May and was serving in Italy, where he was wounded in 1918. Hemingway would turn his wartime experience into his 1929 novel, *A Farewell to Arms*, about an ambulance driver in Italy during World War I. Some of his short stories also featured Nick Adams and other fictional characters who had been wounded in the war.

Still too young even for the ambulance service, sixteen-year-old Walt was desperate to get into action and needed only parental permission to join the Red Cross if he could prove he

Ernest Hemingway in Milan, Italy, in 1918, where he was wounded in the war. The experience provided the background for his famous novel *A Farewell to Arms*. [National Archives]

Red Cross ambulance drivers in Italy during World War I.
[Library of Congress]

was seventeen. Convincing his mother to sign his enlistment papers, Walt altered his birth certificate, changing his birth date from 1901 to 1900. Soon he was in uniform.

In September 1918, Russell and Walt reported for training at the Red Cross facility in a former amusement park on Chicago's South Side. They would spend a week learning to drive ambulances, another on how to repair and assemble cars, and then two weeks on some basic military drills. Walt wouldn't carry a rifle, but after a month's training, he would be ready to head for Europe.

But before he completed his training, Walt got sick. Very sick.

He was taken home by ambulance. For more than three weeks, while his mother cared for him, Walt was flat on his back in bed. He had the flu. By then, Russell and the other young men in his ambulance company had completed their course and shipped out to France. When Walt finally got better, he completed his training, and eventually Walt Disney headed "over there."

FRANKLIN D. ROOSEVELT was also eager to get into a uniform. A thirty-six-year-old assistant secretary of the navy, he was a distant cousin to Theodore Roosevelt. The former president had been one of America's biggest boosters of going to war against Germany.

In his navy post, Franklin had been working to modernize and upgrade America's warships as the United States prepared to join the British and French against Germany. Once America declared war in April 1917, Franklin D. Roosevelt decided that he wanted to fight.

His cousin, the former president, had fought earlier in the Spanish-American War, emerging as a national combat hero. Theodore Roosevelt went on to become America's youngest

The future president of the United States, Franklin D. Roosevelt, as assistant secretary of the navy in 1913. *[Library of Congress]*

president. Franklin had political ambitions of his own. War-time service, he knew, would be a valuable asset when the time came to run for office. But active service was not to be. In his navy position, Franklin went on a tour of American trenches in France in the late summer of 1918.

After touring battlefields in France and visiting his naval counterparts in Italy, Franklin boarded the *Leviathan*, a German passenger ship that had been seized and converted to an American troop carrier. While he may have fallen ill before sailing, Franklin D. Roosevelt got very sick during the ocean crossing. When the *Leviathan* docked, this son of a wealthy New York family was rushed by ambulance to his mother's East Sixty-Fifth Street townhouse and slowly nursed back to health. Ill for weeks, the future president of the United States nearly died. He had the flu.

Walt Disney and Franklin D. Roosevelt were among the lucky ones—the survivors. They lived through the Spanish flu. Franklin D. Roosevelt went on to lead the nation through the Great Depression and World War II, becoming the only American president elected four times. And sixteen-year-old Walt Disney survived the epidemic to become the genius behind Mickey Mouse and the Magic Kingdom.

FOLLOWING PAGES: The *Leviathan* in New York Harbor. *[Wikimedia]*

The enterprising young Walt Disney used this image
on his business envelopes a few years after the war ended.
Of course, he would become the genius behind what
he called "animated motion picture cartoons." [Wikimedia]

This pair had something else in common. Along with
millions of Americans, they had been part of a massive mobilization to fight in Europe's Great War.

When the United States entered World War I, few Americans had ever fought on foreign soil. Protected by oceans,

Americans had largely agreed with George Washington, who said in 1796, "Why . . . entangle our peace and prosperity in the toils of European ambition?"

Since Washington left office, there had been brief forays into North African ports, attacks on Canada during the War of 1812, and a short war with Mexico, and troops had gone to Cuba, the Philippines, and Puerto Rico during the Spanish-American War. American troops had also been deployed to the Caribbean, South America, and again to Mexico. But these had all been limited conflicts.

While Great Britain, France, and their allies slogged through the first few horrendous years of war against Germany and its allies, the United States had remained on the sidelines. Most Americans, including President Woodrow Wilson, were hopeful that diplomacy could keep American lives out of Europe's bloody mess. The Huns might be barbaric, but that was Europe's problem. Besides, there were millions of German Americans who were not eager to see the United States join the fight.

That quickly changed. Spurred by an intercepted German message, President Wilson asked Congress to take the nation into war on April 2, 1917. With an army numbering about 130,000 men, Wilson called for the immediate addition of 500,000 troops. He also wanted Congress to provide "the organization and mobilization of all the material resources of the country to supply the materials of war."

Stirred by Wilson's war call to arms, Americans like Walt Disney and Franklin Roosevelt charged into the conflict. Still largely a country of farmers, the nation rapidly shifted to a wartime footing that transformed American life and turned the nation into an industrial powerhouse. Almost overnight, factories and shipyards began humming in round-the-clock work shifts. Coal and steel production boomed to provide the tanks, planes, and battleships that America needed. Millions of soldiers heading to combat required guns, ammunition, uniforms, blankets, and boots. The millions of immigrants who had flooded into America by the early twentieth century would find plenty of work in these bustling factories and mines.

"Uncle Sam" also wanted Americans—including the newly arrived immigrants—to fill out an army. Six weeks after war was declared, a law was signed requiring men between the ages of twenty-one and thirty to register for military service. Conscription—a military draft—had never been a popular idea among Americans. The law was called the Selective Service Act to soften the fact that the United States was going to draft millions of men into the military.

To get all those men ready for war, thirty-six cantonments, or training camps, sprung up around the country. In these "military boomtowns of tents and barracks," soldiers quickly began preparing for combat, shuttling to other bases before shipping off to Europe.

It was in one of these camps that the Spanish flu emerged.

The first recorded American outbreak took place in early March 1918 at Camp Funston, part of Fort Riley, an old cavalry outpost in Kansas. When the United States entered the war a year earlier, Fort Riley had been expanded to house up to fifty thousand recruits in three thousand hastily constructed barracks and other buildings. Healthy young Americans, many of them fresh off the farm, were brought there to prepare to fight in a foreign war. Many of them thought it was going to be a grand and glorious adventure. But they quickly got a harsh dose of reality.

The camp was on the dusty Kansas prairie, where the Smoky Hill and Republican Rivers meet to form the Kansas River. As the trainees arrived in the middle of an especially cold Kansas winter of 1917–18, they soon learned what soldiers have always known—there was little that was romantic, glorious, or adventurous about life in boot camp.

Crowded into poorly heated, bare wooden barracks, sleeping on cots inches apart, the trainees were often nose-to-nose, with little privacy or breathing room. The barracks couldn't hold the waves of fresh recruits that continued to roll in. Some

were forced to live in simple canvas army tents exposed to the cold. Seeking any warmth, the men often huddled together around woodstoves or open fires.

The first signs of trouble came in the morning on March 4, 1918. A young army private named Albert Gitchell, who served as a company cook, complained of a bad cold. The medical officer who examined him found that Albert's symptoms

U.S. soldiers train for combat. There were thousands
of horses at Camp Funston; the mounted cavalry
was still part of warfare in 1918. [U.S. Army]

included fever, sore throat, headache, and muscle pains—all
typical signs of the flu. The young Gitchell was immediately
quarantined, or set apart from the other soldiers, in a contagion

Receiving field rations at a cantonment. *[Library of Congress]*

ward. Two minutes after Gitchell checked into the infirmary, Corporal Lee Drake arrived with similar complaints. Then a third soldier stumbled in with the same symptoms.

As a cook, Gitchell hadn't been sequestered from the other men in a storeroom or at a desk. He was dead center in the middle of the action, slinging the hash that would be served to hundreds of men in the chow line. With every plate he touched, and every time he coughed or sneezed, Gitchell was potentially infecting the men he served. Soon after he was quarantined, dozens of soldiers reported to the camp doctor with similar complaints. By lunchtime, 107 ailing soldiers had been added to the sick lists. By the end of the week, 522 similar cases had been reported. Within five weeks, more than 1,000 soldiers had fallen ill at Fort Riley, and 46 of them had died.

Military casualties—deaths and battle wounds—are part of the calculus of war. Army doctors prepare for combat injuries such as bullet wounds, bayonet slashes, and amputations in the field. They also know that measles and tuberculosis often hit men in military camps. The spate of deaths they were seeing in Camp Funston was not caused by battle, although they were just as sudden and violent. These sick men were suffering from something far worse than any illness the doctors had ever seen or studied. The flu at Camp Funston was also bringing on pneumonia, a serious infection of the lungs that can be caused by viruses, bacteria, or fungi, which triggers the body's immune system to fight off the infection. In a healthy person, these natural defenses can overcome the pneumonia. But in someone with a weak immune system, the infection cannot be contained. In the lungs are tiny air sacs where oxygen passes into your blood—called the alveoli. As these become infected, they start to fill up with fluid and pus, making it more difficult to breathe. The loss of oxygen can be fatal.

FOLLOWING PAGES: The overcrowded hospital cots at Camp Funston in Fort Riley, Kansas. [National Museum of Health and Medicine, Armed Forces Institute of Pathology]

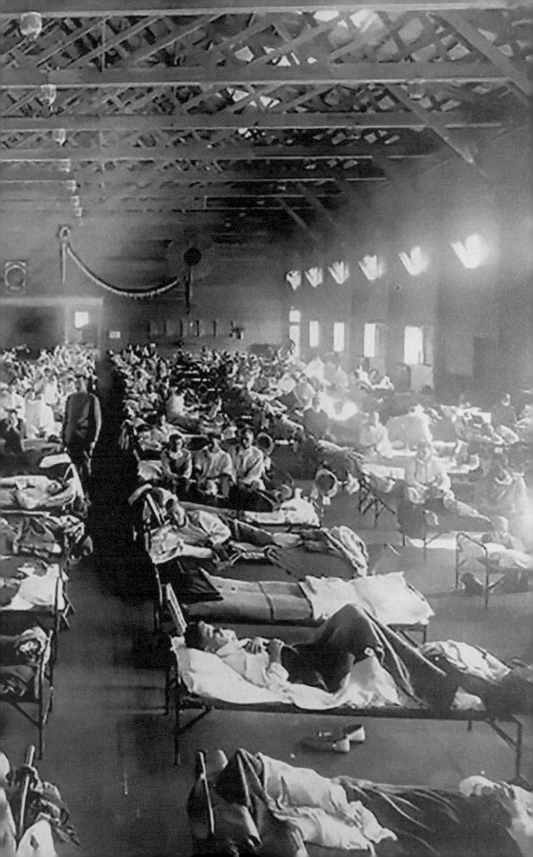

The disease at Camp Funston attacked the lungs. But these cases were extreme—and deadly. Within hours, the men's lungs were filling rapidly with fluid; some were bleeding from their noses.

As young soldiers lay on cots, choking helplessly on their own body fluids, the scene was something out of an end-of-the-world horror movie. Fit when they arrived in camp, these new recruits were suddenly knocked flat on their backs. The contagion ward soon overflowed with new arrivals. The mysterious illness turned these healthy young men blue—a medical condition called cyanosis, in which the skin and membranes take on a blue or purple color from lack of oxygen in the blood. ("Cyanosis" comes from the Greek words *kyanos* for dark blue and *-osis* for disease or condition.)

Most people tend to think of blood as red in color. But if you look at the veins in your wrist, you can see they are blue. Blood without oxygen is blue; human blood turns red when it carries oxygen. The red blood cells receive the needed oxygen when they pass through the lungs. Red blood cells then carry oxygen to be used in the cells found in our bodies. When the lungs cannot transfer oxygen to the blood, cyanosis occurs and the victim turns blue.

In a typical flu outbreak, the illness is most dangerous for the elderly and the very young. These groups are most susceptible because they usually have the weakest immune system—the human body's natural defenses against disease and illness. But the vast majority of deaths at Camp Funston were of seemingly healthy young men who should have gotten over the flu with a few days of bed rest. Instead, they were falling like wheat before the scythe.

The unusual deaths of young men who might be expected to recover from a bout of the flu was one reason the illness hitting the camp seemed so different from typical influenza cases.

To many people, the difference between a bad cold and the flu is hard to tell. The words "cold" and "flu" are often used interchangeably. It is true that both illnesses have some things in common. Both often begin with similar symptoms: coughs, a runny or stuffy nose, chills, and maybe fever. But the flu usually hits a lot harder and drags on longer than the common cold, with fevers, painful body aches, and severe headaches.

Both are caused by viruses. Cold and flu viruses are typically spread by contact with people who are infected—sometimes through shaking hands or touching doorknobs and other objects covered with countless live viruses. But they are mostly shared through coughs and sneezes. And you don't have to kiss or touch, says the CDC. People with flu can spread it to others up to about six feet away.

About three thousand droplets of saliva are expelled in a single cough, and some of them fly out of the mouth at speeds of up to fifty miles per hour. A sick person's cough can contain two hundred million individual virus particles. Sneezing is even more impressive.

"It starts at the back of the throat and produces even more droplets—as many as 40,000—some of which rocket out at speeds greater than 200 miles per hour," according to science writer Jason Socrates Bardi. "The vast majority of the droplets are less than 100 microns across—the width of a human hair."

It's like a video game with space invaders—only there are more of them, flying faster than any computer game can simulate. All those invisible viruses blasting through the air at fantastic high speeds are what spread colds and flu. While there is not yet a cure for either the common cold or the flu, there are now plenty of medicines available to help us deal with the symptoms. Pain and fever reducers may ease discomfort. Modern antiviral drugs may help us recover more quickly and keep the flu from becoming even more dangerous. There are also flu vaccines that may help prevent a serious, or even deadly, case of flu. No such medications existed in 1918. The violent illness that struck Camp Funston—"knock-me-down-fever"—was not only deadly but it was moving to other army and navy bases around the country. And it was moving fast.

Two weeks after the first cases of the mysterious outbreak in Kansas, a rash of illness hit hard at twenty-four of the army's largest camps in March and April. "Today such news would galvanize the Medical Corps," says historian Alfred Crosby, "but in 1918 it attracted only a modicum of attention. There were few similar civilian reports to put alongside the army's and create a picture of a nationwide epidemic."

Besides, there was a war to fight. Soldiers infected with the flu virus didn't have the luxury of staying in bed with cups of chicken soup. The rush to send them to the front lines meant that sick and infected men were jammed elbow to elbow on troop trains and arrived in port cities on crowded transport ships.

By May 1918, a year after the United States entered the war, more than one million American soldiers had been shipped off to France. Known as the American Expeditionary Forces, the U.S troops sent to fight against Germany were under the command of General John J. Pershing. The Great War had already taken millions of European lives. Soldiers from Germany, Italy, Russia, and Great Britain and a host of other countries were in desperate combat on battlefields across the globe—the reason it would be called a "World War."

Now U.S. soldiers were being thrown into deadly trench combat with horrific casualties. As the American "doughboys" began to fight the Germans, there was another enemy, this one unseen. Sent to save the Allied cause, the doughboys carried the deadly flu virus along with their rifles and rucksacks and would set off an explosion.

Soon after these fresh American recruits landed in French ports, the first widespread wave of the flu hit Europe. In April 1918, signs of an epidemic appeared near the French port of Brest, where troop ships carrying 791,000 Americans would land over the course of the war. In May 1918, the illness struck England, where King George V came down with the flu but recovered. Later that month, the king's Grand Fleet was disabled—not by German submarines but by the flu. More than 10,000 sailors, confined in cramped quarters belowdecks, were overcome with high fevers and "the pukes." In the midst of a war, the battleships of the world's mightiest navy could not put out to sea. America's allies, the French and British, had been hit by this crippling new foe.

But it was no better on the German side. Fearing that his country might have to surrender as the Americans reinforced the British and French troops, German General Erich Ludendorff prepared to mount a major offensive in the summer of 1918. Attempting to muster his forces, he had a plan ready to push back the Allies before the American forces could make a difference. A German breakthrough could bring victory. It might change the shifting winds of war.

Then, suddenly, the German advance faltered. "I gather that the epidemic of grippe which hit us rather hard in Flanders also hit the Boche [Germans] rather worse," an American army surgeon wrote in his journal, "and this may have caused the delay."

He was correct. General Ludendorff was unable to marshal the troops necessary to push back the Allied advance. They were too sick to fight. Half a million of General Ludendorff's soldiers had been weakened by what the Germans called Flanders fever.

The flu—not some general's grand strategy—had helped check the German offensive, alter war plans, and influence the course of the war.

Then, almost as mysteriously as this round of flu had appeared in the spring, it seemed to vanish by the early summer of 1918—typical for the end of flu season. In early August, the British army optimistically declared that the epidemic was over.

CHAPTER TWO

THE
SPANISH LADY

It is horrible. One can stand it to see one, two or twenty
men die, but to see these poor devils dropping
like flies sort of gets on your nerves.
—Army doctor in Massachusetts, September 1918

In the morning the dead bodies are stacked about
the morgue like cord wood.
—Dr. Victor Vaughan

T HE THREE-DAY FEVER had broken. As autumn approached, the desperate French and British generals could see a faint glimmer of hope. Germany's June offensive had sputtered. The enemy's advance halted outside Paris. And the Yanks were coming. Americans streamed into France at more than a hundred thousand a month.

"They looked larger than ordinary men; their tall, straight figures were in vivid contrast to the under-sized armies of pale recruits to which we had grown accustomed," wrote Vera Brittain, a young woman nursing the British wounded in France. "I pressed forward with the others to watch the United States physically entering the war, so god-like, so magnificent, so splendidly unimpaired in comparison with the tired,

This recruiting poster, created in 1918 by artist Harry R. Hopps, shows how Germans were depicted in official propaganda aimed at the American public. *[Library of Congress]*

49

nerve-racked men of the British Army. So these were our deliverers at last."

But were these seemingly strong, well-fed Yanks really so "splendidly unimpaired"?

Not at Camp Devens, an army camp outside of Boston, where something was clearly wrong. By late summer, men were again filling the wards with symptoms of the grippe—a common word for influenza.

By September 1918, the full-blown epidemic had returned—more contagious and lethal than before. In a letter to a colleague, a doctor at Camp Devens described the scene:

> They very rapidly develop the most viscous type of Pneumonia that has ever been seen. Two hours after admission they have the Mahogany spots over the cheek bones, and a few hours later you can begin to see the Cyanosis extending from their ears and spreading all over the face, until it is hard to distinguish the coloured men from the white. It is only a matter of a few hours then until death comes.... It is horrible. One can stand it to see one, two or twenty men die, but to see these poor devils dropping like flies sort of gets on your nerves.

FRESH REPORTS OF a second outbreak had surfaced as early as August 19, when the *New York Times* reported, "A considerable number of American negroes, who have gone to France on horse transports, have contracted Spanish influenza on shore and died in French hospitals of pneumonia."

As the *Times* account noted, this strange new illness had been given a name. It came from a Spanish news service cable to Reuters' London office: A STRANGE FORM OF DISEASE OF EPIDEMIC CHARACTER HAS APPEARED IN MADRID. Millions had fallen ill in Spain, including King Alfonso XIII. Spanish newspapers chose to call it the Naples Soldier, after a song in a hit musical playing in Madrid. But much of the world soon began to call this malady the Spanish flu or the Spanish Lady.

In the United States, the first recorded cases of this new, second round of virulent sickness were in Boston. A major supply hub for the war effort, Boston was home to a frenzy of activity as ships delivered both men and materials before they were shipped to Europe. Crowded into a large barracks at the city's Commonwealth Pier were some seven thousand sailors.

On August 27, 1918, a few men reported to sickbay. A day later, there were eight new cases, and by August 29, there were fifty-eight sick men. With the sickbay overwhelmed by feverish sailors, some men were transferred to the U.S. Naval Hospital in nearby Chelsea, Massachusetts. Three medical officers soon fell sick and two of them died.

The onset was sudden, with patients going from healthy to flat on their backs in just hours. It usually began with a spike

"The Final Hour": In Spain, the flu was known as the Naples Soldier.
[Wikimedia]

in temperature to dangerous levels. "Fevers ran from 101° to 105°," historian Alfred Crosby writes, "and the sick complained of general weakness and severe aches in their muscles, joint, backs, and heads. The sufferers commonly described themselves as feeling as if they 'had been beaten all over with a club.'"

Even as the count of men coming down with this new round of illness climbed, thousands of shipyard workers gathered for a parade. During the war, parades became a popular way to boost American morale and trumpet the sale of war bonds. When a patriotic "Win the War for Freedom" march took place in Boston on September 3, it set a match to a barrel of gunpowder.

Within days, the severe illness was racing through the city. From sailors to dockworkers to parade-goers, the contagion jumped from the military to the civilian population. Soon infected civilians began arriving at Boston City Hospital. Then students at the Naval Radio School at Harvard, across the Charles River from Boston, reported sick. On September 8, the first flu deaths were reported in the city.

With America fully at war in the autumn of 1918, soldiers were dying in the blood-soaked muck of European trenches. In

Commonwealth Pier, site of the September 1918 outbreak among sailors in Boston. *[Library of Congress]*

the Meuse-Argonne offensive that began in late September, forty-seven days of fighting would leave twenty-six thousand Americans dead and more than one hundred thousand wounded.

But Americans were also falling at home in numbers never seen before. In large cities and small towns, and across the nation's heartland, America was caught in the relentless grip of a mysterious killer.

As the frightening toll mounted, thousands of men continued to pour into crowded army posts around the country. The recruits, healthy when they arrived at training camps like Camp Devens in Ayer, Massachusetts, soon fell sick. Even as they prepared for the barbed wire and bayonets of Belgium and France, hundreds, and soon thousands, were turning blue, coughing up blood, and dying. Bodies had to be piled like stacks of wood. The overworked doctors and nurses also began to fall sick and drop.

Was this a new plague? Or could it be the Germans?

Ever since the Great War had broken out in August 1914, Americans had heard of terrible atrocities committed by the Germans, who were depicted as merciless barbarians in American posters calling for sacrifice and the sale of war bonds. Accounts of the fighting on front pages of newspapers like the *Washington Post* described German armies as "the Hun." After invading Belgium early in the war, the German army had destroyed Belgian cities, turning thousands of civilians into homeless refugees. Some reports said that German troops had bayoneted French and Belgian babies and cut off boys' hands so they couldn't become soldiers. While atrocities had certainly been committed against civilians, many of these

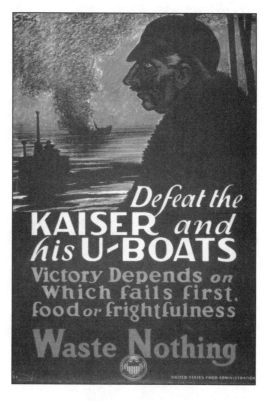

A poster from the United States Food Administration depicts the fear of German U-boats. This federal office was created to organize food and grain from America that was sent to Europe for the troops and starving civilians. Future president Herbert Hoover led the effort and is credited with saving many lives during the war. *[Library of Congress]*

Another World War I poster shows how Germans
were depicted by the American campaign to raise
money through war bonds. *[Library of Congress]*

reports were exaggerated propaganda or what now might be
called "fake news."

But as more Americans dropped dead, the rumors of
German treachery flew fast, spreading around the country.
Had Germany's ruler, the kaiser, ordered his notorious

submarines—or U-boats—to release clouds of poison near American ports? Did the German chemical company Bayer lace aspirin—its "drug of the century"—with a deadly substance? Or had Hun spies spread vials of lethal bacteria in America's water supplies?

Fear gripped the nation as suspicion led to panic. Nobody

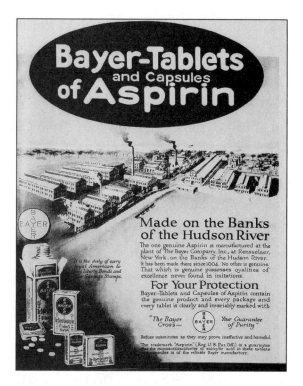

Aspirin was considered a wonder drug when introduced around 1900. In 1917, Bayer lost its U.S. patent on aspirin, and other companies began to produce the drug. The Bayer Company advertised its product to make sure that people knew it was safe and manufactured in America by Americans, not by Germans. *[Library of Congress]*

had seen such violent and gruesome loss of life on such a monumental scale. What was this incredibly deadly disease that struck so suddenly?

Addressing the question were some of America's best doctors. Top medical researchers had been inducted into the army to help prevent contagions from spreading among the troops. As alarming reports flowed in that the Spanish flu had struck Camp Devens, four of them were dispatched to the camp by Army Surgeon General William C. Gorgas. Surgeon General Gorgas knew very well the devastation that contagion could wreak on an army. During the Spanish-American War, he led the successful effort to eradicate yellow fever from Cuba, where the disease wiped out thousands of soldiers.

The group was led by two of the most prominent medical researchers of the day. Seventy-one years old, William Henry Welch was a founder of the Johns Hopkins Hospital in Baltimore and later the Johns Hopkins School of Hygiene and Public Health Medicine; he had joined the U.S. Army Medical Corps in 1917. A survivor of yellow fever in the Spanish-American War, Victor Vaughan was dean of the University of Michigan Medical School and director of the Surgeon General's Office of Communicable Disease. Rufus Cole was the first director of the Rockefeller University Hospital, and the fourth member was Simeon Wallbach of the Harvard Medical School.

All four men were old hands. They understood that disease typically kills more soldiers in wartime than combat does. They had just completed a tour of army bases in the South and left reassured that conditions were good. They also knew of the unusual deaths at Camp Funston in March. But nothing could have prepared them for what they were about to witness.

When the four medical men arrived to inspect Devens, they found unimaginable chaos. A continuous line of infected, gravely ill men snaked into the base hospital. Some carried their blankets; others were being carried, too sick to walk. And the death toll was mounting with uncontrollable speed.

One of the specialists, Dr. Victor Vaughan, had experience with epidemics and had seen how the American army was crippled by typhoid fever in the Spanish-American War. A former president of the American Medical Association, Dr. Vaughan reported, "They are placed on the cots until every bed is full and yet others crowd in. The faces wear a bluish cast; a distressing cough brings up the blood stained sputum." Vaughan was shocked by the conditions at Camp Devens.

Like Camp Funston, Devens had been constructed rapidly after America entered the war. Built by the largest labor force assembled in the United States to that date, it was an entire city, with quarters for the men, water and sewer systems, a hospital, and training facilities. Devens went up at the astonishing

Barracks and troops in training at Camp Devens.

[Fort Devens Museum]

rate of more than ten new buildings every day. Its orderly lines of barracks and buildings had become home to nearly fifty thousand men.

Designed for as many as two thousand men, the hospital at Camp Devens could probably accommodate double that number. But within days, more than *eight thousand* soldiers were lying desperately sick in the hospital. Seventy of the two hundred nurses on duty were also sick, with more falling ill every hour. Urine, feces, and blood were everywhere. Many of the soldiers—healthy, normal young men in their twenties when they arrived in camp—were turning blue, the telltale cyanosis, a deadly sign of death.

And then there were the piles of corpses. They crowded the hallways.

"In the morning the dead bodies are stacked about the morgue like cord wood," Dr. Vaughan said.

His colleague, Dr. William Henry Welch, was one of the world's leading biological investigators. Over a long career, Welch had researched unusual Asian diseases that had never been seen in America. But in all his life, nothing prepared Dr. Welch for the devastation at Devens. Seeing the open chest of an autopsied dead soldier, the mystified veteran researcher grimly told his colleagues, "This must be some new kind of infection or plague."

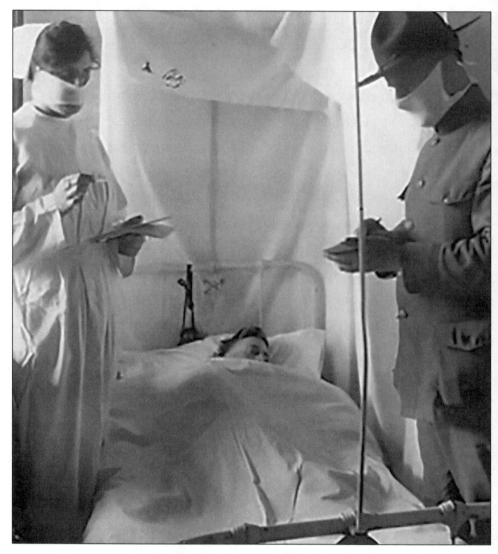

A ward at Camp Devens, one of the hardest hit
army bases in the early days of the pandemic.
[National Archives and Records Administration]

And it had clearly moved well beyond the army bases. Within days of the Camp Devens outbreak, as many as fifty thousand people in Massachusetts had the flu.

Dr. Welch called acting Army Surgeon General Charles Richard and urged that every army camp immediately begin to expand hospital space. Alerting the army leadership, Richard advised them to halt transfers of men in and out of infected camps. "New men will almost surely contract the disease," he wrote. A day later, he added, "The deaths at Camp Devens from influenza and its complications will probably exceed 500." That forecast was too low by far. By late September, the hospital at Camp Devens was averaging about a hundred deaths per day.

The alarm bells were clanging. Yet the dire warnings of all these medical experts would be swept aside. The army leadership and President Wilson wanted no letup in the mobilization. The war effort was front and center. And in fact, it was already too late. The outbreak sweeping through Massachusetts in September was only the tip of a large, catastrophic iceberg.

"I was on duty at Great Lakes [Naval Station] on Friday, September 13, 1918, when I was assigned to a ward of 'flu' patients," recalled James H. Wallace, then a young, inexperienced physician at the navy's main training base near Chicago. "It had struck the training station like a bomb and the 100,000 men there suddenly filled up the hospital's 3,000 beds. I was

assigned to a second ward and then two more wards. I was responsible for about 100 patients, most with violent broncho-
pneumonia.... The death rate was unbelievable, over 100 a
day. At that time, there
was no sulfa, no penicil-
lin, not much but aspi-
rin and, in the hands
of some doctors, whis-
key. The epidemic went
through the camp rap-
idly and fortunately sub-
sided rapidly. I didn't get
sick at all."

The result was dev-
astation on a scale that
is hard to imagine. As
science writer Gina Ko-
lata describes it, "Each
incident, each military
installation that was
struck, each town or city,
each remote village, had
its own monstrous tale of
death, helplessness, and
social collapse."

What had begun as a military crisis was soon an unprecedented public health disaster, reaching into city neighborhoods and country villages around the world.

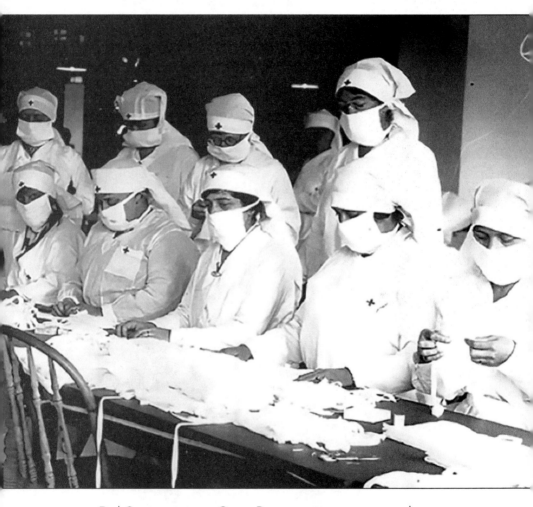

Red Cross nurses at Camp Devens prepare gauze masks for use in the camp. *[National Archives and Records Administration]*

CHAPTER THREE

"BLUE AS HUCKLEBERRIES

AND SPITTING BLOOD"

IF YOU MUST KISS, KISS VIA KERCHIEF
—*New York Sun* headline, August 17, 1918

O N ST. MARK'S PLACE in Manhattan's East Village, a pregnant mother named Rose told her five-year-old son, Joey, to take his baby sister and go to a neighbor to get some food. Rose was lying ill and exhausted beside her sick husband, praying that he would survive. A recent immigrant, she could hear the clopping of the horse cart on the cobblestones outside as it stopped to pick up the dead. It was autumn 1918 and the Spanish flu was raging through New York City's immigrant tenements.

Her neighbor's nineteen-year-old son had already died. But

A streetcar conductor in Seattle refuses a passenger who is not wearing a gauze mask. [National Archives and Records Administration] the rest of the family survived. Once you made it through the "Spanka"—Spanish flu—you were safe.

Back home in Rose's village in Eastern Europe, the scene was much the same. Rose's brother Hersh was sick in bed, as was half of the village. The remote village's only doctor had run away to the Black Sea, saying, "Nothing keeps you healthy like the salt air."

As Rose's mother, Sarah, nursed her ailing son and some of the other villagers, she said, "Can you run away from the Angel of Death? God is punishing the whole world, like the generation of the Flood."

During that dreadful fall of 1918, Rose's mother was soon dead. Her brother Hersh survived. Back in New York, Rose also made it through the Spanka and gave birth to a second son.

From the Lower East Side of Manhattan to the Carpathian Mountains of Eastern Europe, from army bases across America to Arctic fishing villages, the Spanish flu was circling the globe with frightening speed and high mortality rates. Striking with sudden violence, it hit cities, ships at sea, whole armies, and small villages on every continent. From New York's crowded tenements to Native American reservations in South Dakota, the Spanish Lady recognized no boundaries or divisions of race or social status—although the poorest, as is often true, suffered the most.

Its victims included presidents and princes, poets and

painters. Rose Cleveland, sister of former President Grover Cleveland and who had once served as first lady, died of the flu. So did playwright Edmond Rostand, author of *Cyrano de Bergerac*, poet Guillaume Apollinaire, and Austrian artist Egon Schiele.

Leopold S. Kahn, a dwarf featured in P. T. Barnum's famed circus as Admiral Dot, fell victim. So did a German immigrant to America who had made a small fortune opening hotels and saloons for miners in the Yukon gold rush. He later returned to New York, where in May 1918, Frederick Trump—grandfather of Donald Trump—was walking down the street when he felt sick and suddenly died of pneumonia brought on by the flu.

The world's richest woman at the time, silent screen star Mary Pickford, fell seriously ill but survived. Lillian Gish, another of Hollywood's greatest stars of the silent film era, also lived through the flu. So did poet Robert Frost and Edvard Munch, the Norwegian artist famed for *The Scream*.

The pandemic was taking millions of lives. So was the war, and everything was changing.

On the American home front, as millions of men went off to fight, women were often left alone to take care of farms and families. Some took jobs on production lines in factories, now crowded with workers in round-the-clock shifts to keep up with the insatiable demands of a booming military. From

With P. T. Barnum's Traveling World's Fair.
ADMIRAL DOT.
Sixteen years old; Twenty-five inches high.
Weighs only Nineteen pounds.

A famous performer in P. T. Barnum's circus, the man known as Admiral Dot was one of the people who died during the Spanish flu pandemic in America. *[Wikimedia]*

uniforms and pistol parts to tanks and airplanes, these factories were producing America's arsenal.

Outside of factories, some women enlisted as Red Cross nurses or volunteered to roll bandages that would be needed at the front. Eager to serve, hundreds of other women joined the Salvation Army, volunteering for duty in France. Beloved by the doughboys, these intrepid "Sallies" sewed buttons and gave treasured moral support to men at the front. They also served doughnuts. According to Salvation Army tradition, two women volunteers—Ensign Margaret Sheldon and Adjutant Helen Purviance—couldn't bake properly at the front and

Edvard Munch: *Self Portrait after Spanish Influenza* (1919).
[Nasjonalmuseet, The Fine Art Collections / Høstland, Børro / Creative Commons]

The war meant that many women went to work in factories as men were called up for military service. These women inspect automatic pistol parts at a plant in Hartford, Connecticut. *[Library of Congress]*

began to fry dough in soldiers' helmets. The nickname "doughboy" for soldier was an old one that predates 1917, but it became attached to the American soldiers serving in World War I. The popularity of the Salvation Army "doughnut lassies" sealed the connection.

At the same time across America, fund-raising became a national obsession, fueled by propaganda. Warfare is very expensive, both in "blood and treasure"—an old expression for the high cost of war in lives and money. During America's two years of preparation for combat and fighting, the cost to the United States was an estimated $32 billion dollars, an extraordinary amount of money in 1918.

To meet these staggering costs, Americans were whipped

Salvation Army volunteers served coffee and doughnuts, sewed buttons, and kept up the spirits of the "doughboys" in France.
[Salvation Army Metropolitan Division]

into a near frenzy by government propaganda. Rich and poor alike, American citizens were cajoled and pressured to buy bonds from the government as a way to pay for the costly war effort. A bond, such as the saving bonds offered by the U.S. Treasury today, is essentially a government's way to borrow money. It is a loan made to the government with the promise of repayment with interest. War bonds, called Liberty Loans, were specifically designed to pay for these large military costs.

The bonds were promoted by silent movie celebrities like Charlie Chaplin, who even made a promotional propaganda movie called *The Bond*.

It may be difficult today to understand how intense the pressure was during this Liberty Loan drive. But on the American home front during World War I, anyone who was accused of failing to "do their part" or being a "slacker" faced the criticism of friends and neighbors, or worse. A volunteer group called the American Protective League was given semiofficial status by the Justice Department. Numbering some two hundred thousand and wearing badges that said "Secret Service," members spied on neighbors, investigated slackers and food hoarders, and demanded to know why people didn't buy bonds.

Selling bonds was the most visible way to keep American morale high and rally support for war. Large parades to

Douglas Fairbanks holds Charlie Chaplin aloft at a Wall Street bond rally in 1918. The two men were among the most famous silent screen actors of the time. *[Underwood & Underwood, The New York Times]*

promote the war bonds were a high priority. Of course, parades meant crowds. And many illnesses, including influenza, are crowd diseases: they flourish and spread when people are together in large numbers.

A September 1918 parade by thousands of workers had taken place in Boston, only to be followed by a flu explosion there. Later that month, Philadelphia decided to strike up the band and put on its own rousing show of war support. Philadelphia's march brought more than two hundred thousand people into the streets on September 28. Within days, the Spanish flu began its own march through the City of Brotherly Love, claiming more than seven thousand lives in a few weeks.

As ports near military bases, both Philadelphia and Boston were slammed hard by the flu. But they were far from

Within days of Philadelphia's Liberty Loan parade in September 1918, which was attended by 200,000 people, hundreds of cases of influenza were reported. [Naval Historical Center]

exceptions. Chicago, Denver, Minneapolis, and other big cities were all coping with similar waves of death. San Francisco had put strong quarantine rules in place in the spring and early autumn of 1918, but they were later relaxed. When this California port city—home of large West Coast military facilities—thought it was in the clear, the flu came roaring back in November. It was no different north of the border, where Canadian cities such as Montreal saw their dead piled onto streetcars in public spectacles of death and despair.

In New York, then the nation's largest city with a population of more than 5.5 million people, the epidemic was slow to take hold at first. Initially, the official reaction was denial or at least to diminish the risks. The health commissioner advised against kissing, "except through a handkerchief." City residents were cautioned not to spit in public and to avoid sharing cups and other eating utensils. When twenty-five people with the Spanish flu were removed from a ship arriving in New York in September, the city's health commissioner reassured the *New York Times* that "none of them was very ill." The *Times* headline proclaimed on September 13 that New York was "not in danger from Spanish grip."

But in a city filled with crowded tenements, busy subways and streetcars, and sailors and soldiers flooding its bustling docks, the flu was waiting to explode. After the Spanish flu made its debut in New York, the city's hospitals were quickly deluged. A doctor in New York's Presbyterian Hospital described a surge of new arrivals there and reported, "They're as blue as huckleberries and spitting blood."

In New York, reports of flu on arriving ships had surfaced in the newspapers since August, but the first diagnosed cases originating in the city were three merchant marine sailors on leave in mid-September. Just a few weeks later, by November 1918, the U.S. Public Health Service reported more than twenty thousand deaths in New York City.

Attempting to slow the spread of this plague, health officials issued a set of aggressive measures. Ships entering New York's busy port were quarantined until they could be declared free of disease. At railroad stations, travelers were stopped, and anyone with signs of flu was banned from public transportation. The "filthy habit"—spitting in public—was made illegal and subject to fines. On October 4, 134 men had to pay $1 at Jefferson Market Court and another three at the Yorkville Court for spitting on subways, subway platforms, and elevated trains.

New York's schools remained open—unlike those in Philadelphia—but mothers sent their children off to classes wearing the cheesecloth masks that were thought to protect against the illness. Classrooms must have had a distinctive aroma as many children also appeared with garlands of garlic cloves draped around their necks—an old folk remedy meant to ward off disease.

"New York is a great cosmopolitan city and in some homes there is careless disregard for modern sanitation," the health commissioner told the *Times*. "In the schools the children are under the constant guardianship of the medical inspectors. This work is part of our system of disease control. If the schools were closed at least 1,000,000 would be sent to their homes and become 1,000,000 possibilities for the disease."

While children went to school, the overflowing crowds crushed hospitals, where doctors, nurses, and other medical staff began to fall ill. At the city's famous Bellevue hospital, one intern later told a reporter, "It got to the place where I would only see patients twice. Once when they came in—and again when I signed the death certificate."

Eventually, New York would see more than thirty thousand deaths from the flu pandemic. The number was high, but the city's strict measures, world-class medical facilities, and recent experience with public health crises, including a bout of polio and a typhoid fever scare, brought about by an Irish cook later known as Typhoid Mary (See Appendix 1), probably prevented disaster on a much greater scale.

Large cities were groaning under the siege of Spanish flu. But so were small towns and rural places. In Tucson, Arizona, the board of health passed a rule saying, "No person shall appear in any street, park, or place where any business is transacted, or in any other public place within the city of Tucson, without

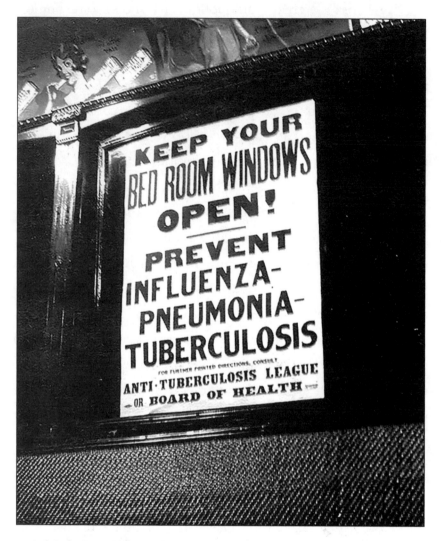

Although some medical experts disagreed, many people treating Spanish flu victims came to the conclusion that fresh air was best for preventing the spread of the disease. [Cincinnati Historical Society]

wearing a mask consisting of at least four thicknesses of butter cloth, or at least seven thicknesses of ordinary gauze, covering both the nose and the mouth."

In El Paso, Texas, poor Mexican migrant workers died at alarming rates, requiring the conversion of a small school into an influenza hospital. On October 19, the local newspaper reported, "Fifty-one Mexican men, women, and babies lay gasping in the improvised wards of Aoy School last night."

Places far removed from the ports where the Spanish flu had reared its head offered no refuge. In Alliance, Nebraska, the Red Cloud family—relatives of the prominent Oglala leader Chief Red Cloud—had just finished picking potatoes at the end of October 1918 when they were told that a sickness was coming and that they should start for their home at the Pine Ridge reservation in South Dakota. Every day they watched wagons go to the graveyard to bury soldiers and those who had died from the flu.

Just as they started to break camp, flu hit the family. But good sense, sound instincts, and excellent nursing provided some ray of hope. On the journey home, grandmother Nancy Red Cloud placed everyone who was sick in their own tent. She boiled a big bucket of flat cedar tea and took it from tent to tent to fill individual cups, making sure there was no sharing of personal items like washbasins or utensils. She burned sweetgrass so the sick could breathe better and "to ward-off evil

Many Native American communities, which were often underserved by doctors or nurses, attempted a form of healing ritual that came to be known as "jingle dress dances." [Manataka American Indian Council]

spirits." To relieve the severe coughs, Nancy Red Cloud fed everyone a teaspoon of kerosene and sugar mixed together. All the Red Cloud family survived.

"In her desperation," her great-great-granddaughter Vanessa Short Bull explains, "Nancy had applied the [principles] of quarantine, prevented cross-contamination, provided hydration and inhalation therapy, and used pharmacology to save her family."

In other Native American communities and reservations, where modern medical facilities were typically substandard at best and often nonexistent, women began to perform the jingle dress dance to promote healing.

The Red Cloud family was fortunate. Dances, home remedies of kerosene and sugar, and dangerous "snake oil" medications sold on the streets rarely helped the most desperately ill. But medical doctors weren't of much more use either. They had few medicines that worked on the flu virus—and many were still not sure it was the flu. Many simply relied on whiskey.

In Lusk, Wyoming, a country doctor boasted that he had never lost a patient. "His secret weapon was 'rotgut' whiskey," recounts Margarita Pancake, whose father lived through the pandemic. "He would pour the whiskey into a patient to get them to cough up the phlegm. During the pandemic, he ran out of whiskey and there was none to be had in the community. The only whiskey in Lusk was locked-up in the sheriff's office as evidence for a bootlegger's trial. The sheriff refused to release the liquor. So, the doctor got a few prominent citizens together for a kind of vigilante committee that promptly seized the whiskey, depriving the sheriff of his evidence."

As America's plague spread in the fall, President Wilson was largely silent on the epidemic, focused instead on the war effort. Once reluctant to take America into Europe's deadly conflict, Wilson used an iron will to harness American energy and mobilize the nation. His single-minded fervor to win what had become a crusade far exceeded his fears of influenza. As the American forces were pressed on to the front lines, Wilson wanted to keep up the pressure on the German foe.

If the war was about saving the future of democracy, as Wilson said it was, the president was going to make sure that total victory was the only outcome. Flu or no flu, the Liberty Loan drives continued. Recruitment efforts went on without letup. The frenzied pace of wartime production raced faster and faster in American coal mines, shipyards, and the factories turning out tanks, rifles, and military uniforms.

But something had changed. Europe's Great War had started in August 1914, but by September 1918, as many soldiers were dying from illness as were lost in combat. On both sides, men were too sick to fight. "If it was difficult to control crowding in the training camps, it was impossible in the battlefields," writes Carol R. Byerly in a history of the flu in the army. "As soldiers in the trenches became sick, the military evacuated them from the front lines and replaced them with healthy men. This process continuously brought the virus into contact with new hosts—young, healthy soldiers in which it could adapt, reproduce, and become extremely virulent without danger of burning out."

American General John Pershing fell ill with the flu but stubbornly pressed for more troops. "Influenza exists in epidemic form amongst our troops in many localities in France accompanied by many serious cases of pneumonia," he wrote as he asked for fifteen hundred more nurses, while also requesting more troops and hospitals.

Then one man did something extraordinary. Army Provost Marshal General Enoch Crowder made a shocking announcement. He canceled the draft call of 142,000 men on September 26. Despite President Wilson and General Pershing calling for more men, Crowder canceled the October draft call as well. He knew that the disease was overwhelming the army. It could not properly train its new soldiers if they were all falling ill. Virtually every army camp to which recruits would report was under quarantine.

The draft may have been put on hold and slowed the pace of adding more trainees, but the pipeline of trainees already in camps was full and the United States continued to send boatloads of young men to Europe—dispatching them to the trenches that would see so much killing. But before they even left those troop ships, they faced death. "The transports," writes historian John M. Barry, "became floating caskets."

FOLLOWING PAGES: Members of the American Expeditionary Force in an influenza ward at U.S. Army Camp Hospital No. 45 in Aix-Les-Bains, France. [U.S. Army Medical Corps, National Museum of Health & Medicine]

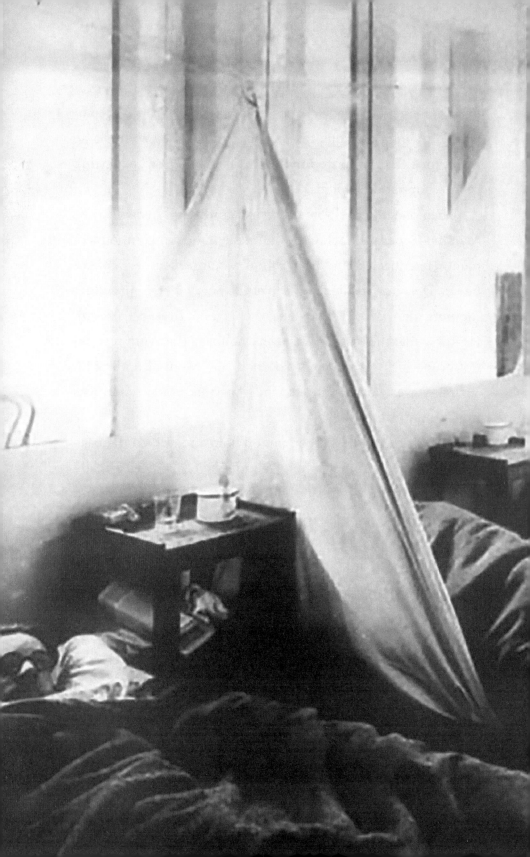

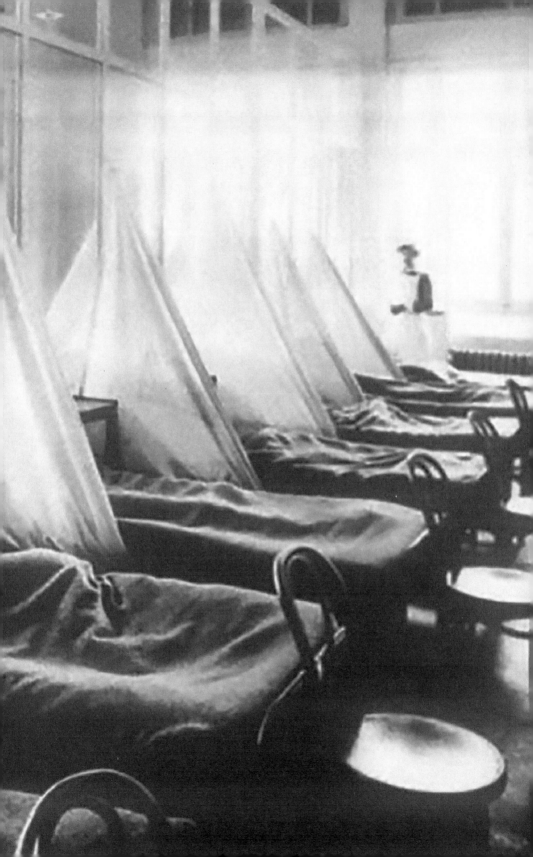

CHAPTER FOUR

"OVER THE TOP"

A Brief History of World War I

I wish those people who write so glibly about this being a holy War . . . could see a case—to say nothing of 10 cases—of mustard gas in its early stages—could see the poor things burnt and blistered all over with great mustard-coloured suppurating blisters, with blind eyes . . . and always fighting for breath, with voices a mere whisper, saying that their throats are closing and they know they will choke.
—Vera Brittain, *Testament of Youth*, 1915

"FIX BAYONETS."

Two words passed down the line. The time had come for going "over the top."

For hours, the men had waited in the predawn darkness as the big guns did their work. Thousands of shells screeched across the pockmarked wasteland—fired by the Germans' massive Big Berthas, some of them miles distant. The sound was deafening, and the earth shook with the tremendous explosions.

"Louder and louder grew the sound of the guns," one British soldier wrote of an artillery barrage. "As if all the gods in heaven were beating on drums the size of lakes."

American troops prepare to go "over the top."
[Library of Congress]

That was 1914, but it might as well have been 1918—so little had changed on this stalemated battlefront. The soldiers stood, nervously, waiting in the muddy, rat-infested, water-filled trenches that were dug at least six feet below the ground. Leaning on their guns, some men tried to shut their eyes and doze. But sleep was impossible. Others smoked a last cigarette before the charge. Some shivered—fighting the cold and fear—knowing what was to come.

The worst was the panicked cry: "Gas!" The warning of a chemical attack meant scrambling to put on the clumsy face-mask before inhaling the mustard gas or chlorine that had become every soldier's most feared threat.

Then came the shrill tweet of the whistles. That was the signal. Quickly, the soldiers began to clamber up shaky wooden ladders. A few never made it past the upper rungs, cut down by enemy guns before they could leave the trench.

Once out of the dugouts, the soldiers followed their commanders. Officers wearing gloves and neckties—as if heading off to a dinner party instead of war—waved pistols and implored the men to move.

The deadly race was on, across hundreds of yards of no-man's-land. The troops ran over what had been farm fields,

A French trench at Verdun, 1916. The trenches were often cold, rat-infested, filled with lice, and muddy. [Wikimedia]

now scarred with craters, deep, muddy holes filled with water, dead horses, and the bodies of the fallen soldiers. From the opposing trenches came a hail of fire—machine guns, rifles, hand grenades, and mortars. If they managed to pass this curtain of death, the men knew that savage hand-to-hand combat waited.

"We are insensible, dead men, who through some trick, some dreadful magic, are still able to run and to kill," German war veteran Erich Maria Remarque wrote in his classic novel, *All Quiet on the Western Front*. "A young Frenchman lags behind, he is overtaken, he puts up his hands, in one he still holds his revolver. . . . A blow from a spade cleaves through his face. A second sees it and tries to run farther; a bayonet jabs into his back. He leaps in the air, his arms thrown wide, his mouth wide open, yelling; he staggers, in his back the bayonet quivers."

THE BLOODY PATH to what had become a futile deadlock began in August 1914. Answering the kaiser's call to fight for the fatherland, German troops forced their way into Belgium, Luxembourg, and France. In response, French armies struck out for the Alsace-Lorraine region, a former French territory controlled by Germany. In support of its Belgian ally, the United Kingdom sent its British Expeditionary Force across the channel. Hundreds of miles to the east, Russian troops prepared to attack Germany and its ally, the empire of Austria-Hungary.

In all, six million men set out across Europe in the late summer of 1914. "It was the largest mass movement of men and

During the years of fighting, trenches sometimes changed hands. This was a German trench occupied by British soldiers in July 1916 during the Battle of the Somme, one of the most deadly battles of the war and in all human history. *[Wikimedia]*

arms ever seen," writes historian Adam Hochschild. "Between countries in the world's industrial heartland, limited war was no longer possible. Total war, of a sort not seen before, was about to begin."

With a few exceptions, including France, many European nations at the time were monarchies, and many members of Europe's royal houses were relatives, linked by bloodlines and marriage. The war and the slaughter were born, in part, out of raging family feuds.

That is one of the reasons this conflict seems so perplexing and pointless. The war was principally declared and led by three monarchs who had met as children and been together in Berlin for the wedding of the German kaiser's daughter in 1913. Kaiser Wilhelm II and Great Britain's King George V were cousins, both grandsons of the late Queen Victoria of Great Britain. The Russian czar was also George's cousin, and his wife was also a granddaughter of Victoria.

Over time, these kinships of blood and marriage had frayed. Personal animosities were worsened by competition for valuable territory—both in Europe and around the world, the growing threat of revolutions, and an extreme level of nationalism accompanied by powerful feelings of superiority. It was an era when competing dreams of world empires destroyed hopes of peaceful negotiation or compromise. Demonstrating

the depths of antago-
nism felt for Germany in
England, the king of the
United Kingdom changed
the family name in 1917
from the German House of
Saxe-Coburg-Gotha to the
House of Windsor.

In the heady first days
before the fighting began,
patriotism and pride filled
the air in all the warring
nations. The British and
French shouted, "To Berlin!"
The Germans shouted, "To
Paris!" Haughty, arrogant,
and supremely confident in
their military power, their
leaders promised a brief
fight and a quick peace.
Some pledged in August
1914 that the troops would
return victorious by Christmas. The kaiser told his

Kaiser Wilhelm II, in 1905, was known
as the all highest warlord.
[Wikimedia]

Great Britain's King George V and Russia's Czar Nicholas II
attended the wedding of the German kaiser's daughter
in Berlin in 1913. *[Library of Congress]*

soldiers, "You will be home before the leaves have fallen from the trees."

Wars often begin with such optimistic predictions. But

after more than four years of back-and-forth fighting and unfathomable losses, the zigzagging lines of trenches nearly 475 miles long had barely moved.

Facing off across those stark battle lines were many young soldiers, often no more than boys from farms and factory floors. Some had left lecture halls and school desks and, after a few weeks of training, wore crisp new uniforms and carried weapons. They were fighting for the fatherland or "God, king, and country," urged on by admiring crowds and girls who tossed flowers as they marched off.

"We had bonded together into one large and enthusiastic group," German veteran Ernst Jünger later wrote. "We shared a yearning for danger, for the experience of the extraordinary. We were enraptured by war. We had set out in a rain of flowers, in a drunken atmosphere of blood and roses. Surely the war had to supply us with what we wanted; the great, the overwhelming, the hallowed experience. We thought of it as manly, as action, a merry duelling party on flowered, blood-bedewed meadows."

Nineteen-year-old Ernst was not unique. He had joined other young Germans who volunteered for duty in August 1914 when Kaiser Wilhelm II ordered the mobilization of German troops. Young men like Ernst viewed going to war as if it were a picnic outing with a holiday mood. Adoring crowds cheered the young soldiers parading through the streets.

Within weeks of the war's outbreak, the stunning human cost of modern warfare became a hideous reality. "In a single day, August 22, the French lost 27,000 men," historian Russell Freedman records, "most of them shot dead by machine guns and long-range rifles or blown to bits by shrapnel and high explosives."

In those first weeks, the kaiser's optimism seemed justified. Germany's disciplined and well-equipped troops struck quickly, roaring through neutral Belgium, expecting to deliver a swift knockout. Although they met with unexpected resistance from a small Belgian army, the Germans captured the Belgian capital of Brussels on August 20, 1914. The first recorded atrocities soon followed as thousands of Belgian civilians were shot under the pretext of having been snipers.

In late August the Germans burned the centuries-old university town of Leuven to the ground, destroying priceless medieval manuscripts along with private homes. Describing the destruction of the ancient and beautiful town, veteran American war correspondent Richard Harding Davis reported, "Opposite was the Church of St. Pierre, dating from the fifteenth century, a very noble building, with many chapels filled with carvings of the time of the Renaissance in wood, stone and iron. In the university were 150,000 volumes. . . . Statues, pictures, carvings, parchments, archives—all are gone."

The German army then wheeled toward Paris, preparing

The ancient university town of Leuven was almost completely destroyed by the German army in August 1914. *[University of Manchester]*

to complete a decisive, sudden victory. As German forces neared the French capital, the panicked French government fled. French generals drew up plans to blow up bridges and the famed Eiffel Tower, then used as an army radio transmitting station. Before the explosives were detonated, however, the French forces and their British allies stiffened their resistance and launched a counterattack.

Desperately using every tool at his disposal, a French general is said to have commandeered Parisian taxicabs to rush reinforcements to the front, thirty miles east of the capital. Over a week's time in September 1914, more than two million men fought in the farmlands around the Marne River near Paris. In this first battle of the Marne, or what the French called the Miracle of the Marne, the German advance was pushed back.

Many miles to the east, in what is now Poland, the czarist Russian army had joined the action. Allied with the French and British against Germany, Russia unexpectedly launched its first offensive just two weeks after the war's outbreak. Clashing in the battle of Tannenberg in late August 1914, 230,000 Russian troops were sent reeling backward by a German force of more than 160,000 men—a complete and humiliating defeat of the Russians. But even as it celebrated its convincing early victories, Germany was weakened. It would now be forced to fight the war on two fronts.

"Germany's resources were simply insufficient to fulfill its towering ambitions in France while conducting simultaneous operations of any kind in the East," notes war historian Max Hastings. "Germany's Tannenberg triumph was also a disaster

A legendary "Marne" taxi used to move French troops
to the battlefield outside of Paris. [Musée de l'Armée, Paris]

for its leaders and for those of its people who craved peace and hoped for an early negotiated end of the struggle."

About a month after the Marne battle, the fighting moved to Ypres in Flanders, Belgium, for the first of several epic battles there. Many of the Germans who fought at Ypres were teenagers, boys fresh from school like Ernst Jünger. Unprepared for the carnage that awaited them, some of them arrived to fight in their school caps. "They were mowed down in their thousands by British rifles and machine guns," records Russell Freedman, "in what became known in Germany as the *Kindermord bei Ypern*, literally 'the Murder of the Children at Ypres.'"

On all sides, the enormous casualties at Marne, Flanders, and other battles left people in shock. And it had only just begun.

Thousands of Russian prisoners and guns were captured at Tannenberg in a complete rout of the Russian army by the Germans in August 1914. *[Wikimedia]*

The scene of the battlefield at Flanders, soon to be immortalized in John McCrae's poem "In Flanders Fields." *[Frank Hurley, Wikimedia]*

The opposing armies began digging the trenches that would become the hallmark of the Great War. Visions of quick conquest were shattered by the bewildering death toll. In just five months, from August 1914 to the end of the year, a million men had been killed, and casualties on all fronts topped five million.

BUT WHAT WAS IT all about? What lit the fuse?

It began with an assassination—the deaths of two somewhat obscure members of a royal house in a somewhat obscure city in Eastern Europe.

On June 28, 1914, Archduke Francis Ferdinand, the fifty-year-old heir to the throne of the Austro-Hungarian Empire, was in Sarajevo in Bosnia, a province annexed by Austria-Hungary in 1908. His wife, Duchess Sophie, accompanied him even though there was a dangerous political mood in the city. Sarajevo was a simmering stew of resentments stirred by Bosnian nationalists who thought the region should be linked to neighboring Serbia.

Eager to break away from Austria, a group of young nationalist students plotted to kill the archduke and spark a rebellion that would win Bosnia its independence. Early that day one of them tossed a grenade at the archduke's motorcade, but the couple escaped harm. Later one of the student plotters happened to see the royal couple's car, which had made a wrong turn and stalled while backing out of an alley. The young

Bosnian shot the archduke and Sophie at point-blank range, killing both. The assassin was captured, and soon tried and convicted. Too young to be executed, nineteen-year-old Gavrilo Princip was sent to prison, where he died of tuberculosis in April 1918.

The assassination set off a fall of dominoes across the map of Europe that historian Adam Hochschild describes as "a powder keg of jostling empires."

"Even today," he adds, "it seems extraordinary how swiftly Princip's two bullets, fired in a city most people had never heard of, set in motion events that would so profoundly reshape our world."

Within days of the death of the archduke and his wife, the "dogs of war" had been set loose. The Austro-Hungarian Empire declared war on Serbia, Austria's tiny neighbor to the south, claiming it was responsible for the assassination. Allied to Serbia, Russia mobilized its troops. Austria's ally Germany responded by

The nineteen-year-old assassin Gavrilo Princip in a 1914 prison photo. [Wikimedia]

declaring war on Russia and its ally, France. Also bound by defense treaties, Great Britain declared war on Germany as German troops began an invasion of Belgium on their way to France.

Like a wildfire leaping from tree to tree in an old, dry forest, the conflagration spread across Europe, sweeping everything in its path. Complicating the picture was the approaching Bolshevik revolution in Russia, which would eventually topple the Russian czar.

Many of these European dynasties and other nations had been itching for a fight. They had all ramped up munitions production, which did wonders for the industrial makers of bullets, bombs, and battleships. The time-honored traditions of sabers and cavalry assaults had given way to such inventions as mustard gas and high-powered explosives. Flamethrowers, tanks, and a new generation of hand grenades and water-cooled machine guns increased the killing power. At sea, powerful, turbine-driven battleships called dreadnoughts ruled above the water, and submarines—such as the German U-boats—did their deadly work from below.

In Europe's capitals, the war cries were fueled by fierce nationalism, complicated alliances, and ancient antagonisms. Cooler heads and gentlemanly diplomacy might have prevailed. But that hope was lost to enormous egos, hotheads with a belief in their armies' invincibility, and nineteenth-century ideals of honor, in an era when leaders did not realize the awesome killing power of their modern weapons. In battles that have become military legend, the human toll was ghastly. Marne. Ypres. Gallipoli. Verdun. Somme. Argonne Forest. Soon these fields and plains sprouted forests of crosses.

While the worst of this deadly fighting was concentrated in Europe, the real prize was elsewhere. Each nation wanted to expand its empire, seizing the spoils of victory in Africa, Asia,

HMS *Dreadnought.* [*U.S. Naval Historical Center*]

and the Middle East. The natural resources and material wealth—South Africa's gold and diamonds, the metals and rubber of Africa, the rubber of Malaysia, the oil of the Mideast— were at the heart of the conflict. As fighting spread to many colonial outposts around the globe, a European war quickly became a world war.

Through the early years of fighting, the United States

remained on the sidelines. Protected by two oceans, Americans were unwilling to get caught in the carnage. Neutralism and isolationism were powerful forces in the United States. A good deal of the population was descended from the countries now at one another's throats. Eight million German Americans had no desire to see America at war with Germany. Another 4.5 million Irish Americans held no desire to fight for

The *Lusitania* arrives at Pier 54 in New York City in 1908.
[Library of Congress]

Great Britain, then tightening its grip on an Ireland struggling for its independence.

Early in May 1915, the German embassy in Washington published advertisements in American newspapers warning Americans to avoid sailing on British ships crossing the Atlantic. On May 7, 1915, a German U-boat off the coast of Ireland torpedoed the British liner *Lusitania*—one of the fastest ocean liners in service. In only eighteen minutes, the huge ship went down, taking with it 1,198 of its 1,959 passengers and crew. Among the dead were 128 Americans.

The sinking of the *Lusitania* enraged the American public and war hawks such as former President Theodore Roosevelt. But President Wilson resisted the loud outcry to strike back at Germany. Instead, he dealt with the Germans through a series of diplomatic notes, demanding reparations and German promises to end passenger ship attacks. Wilson told one of his close aides, "Were I to advise radical action now, we should have nothing, I am afraid, but regrets and heartbreaks."

In his quest for a second term, Woodrow Wilson maintained America's neutrality and campaigned in 1916 under the Democratic slogan "He kept us out of war." Wilson won a close race. But the peace was short-lived. On January 31, 1917, Germany announced it would resume unlimited submarine warfare against all merchant shipping, including American ships.

Wilson broke off diplomatic relations three days later but stopped short of requesting a declaration of war.

The crucial change came with the revelation of the Zimmermann telegram, a coded message sent by the German foreign minister to the German ambassador in Mexico. After British agents intercepted and decrypted it, they turned it over to the United States on February 24. The cable revealed that

During the 1916 presidential race, Democrat Woodrow Wilson campaigned with the slogan "He kept us out of war." A month after Wilson was inaugurated for his second term, the U.S. declared war on Germany. *[Library of Congress]*

Germany was proposing an alliance with Mexico, promising that Mexico would regain territory it had earlier lost to America— including Texas, New Mexico, and Arizona.

The American press published these secret plans on March 1, 1917, just as Germany stepped up its attacks on U.S. ships. On March 18, there was news that the Germans had sunk three American ships. Enraged Americans demanded war.

The stated reasons for America's declaration of war were freedom of the seas and, in the words of Woodrow Wilson, to make the world "safe for democracy." To his credit, Wilson had tried to restrain both sides and mediate a peace.

When Congress declared war on April 6, 1917, America had a small army and navy, no tanks, and very few aircraft. As a sign of American support, a small advance force was sent to France immediately. Symbolically arriving in Paris on July 4, they were led by their commander, General John "Black Jack" Pershing. The general or one of his military aides supposedly said, "Lafayette, we are here," in tribute to the heroic young Frenchman who had become one of the greatest heroes of the American Revolution when he fought alongside George Washington.

America was now in the thick of the war. The next year would see massive nationwide mobilization as Americans prepared to take up the fight. That meant quickly expanding the training facilities at places like Camp Funston in Kansas and Camp Devens in Massachusetts. In these camps, the future doughboys would be introduced to life in the modern army.

They would also be introduced—fatefully—to the Spanish flu.

Milestones in World War I

1914

June 28 Austria's Crown Prince, Archduke Francis Ferdinand, and his wife are murdered in the city of Sarajevo. Following the assassination, the Austro-Hungarian government declares war on Serbia, its tiny southern neighbor. Russia begins to mobilize its troops in defense of Serbia.

August 1 Allied with Austria, Germany declares war on Russia. Two days later, Germany declares war on France.

August 4 Bound by mutual defense treaties, Great Britain declares war on Germany.

August 5 The United States formally declares its neutrality and offers to mediate the growing conflict.

August 23 Japan declares war on Germany.

1915

May 7 The British ocean liner *Lusitania* is sunk by a German U-boat, with more than one hundred Americans among the dead. Germany claims that the liner carried munitions; the British deny this.

December 7 U.S. President Woodrow Wilson requests a standing army of 142,000 and reserves of 400,000.

1916

November Campaigning under the slogan "He kept us out of war" while preparing the nation for entrance into the war on the Allied side, Woodrow Wilson narrowly wins a second term.

1917

April 2 After more American ships are sunk, President Wilson asks Congress to declare war on Germany.

June 24 General John J. Pershing leads the first contingent of Americans, the American Expeditionary Force, to France.

1918

January 8 President Wilson outlines an attempt to settle the war called the Fourteen Points for Peace.

March The first cases of Spanish flu appear among army recruits in Kansas. Within months, every continent and country is affected.

September 26 More than one million Allied troops, including 896,000 Americans, join for an offensive in the last major battle of the war. At the same time, British forces farther north crack the German line of defense, the Hindenburg Line.

November 11 Armistice Day: Fighting ends as a cease-fire treaty, or armistice, is signed and goes into effect at the "eleventh hour of the eleventh day of the eleventh month."

1919

June 28 The Treaty of Versailles is signed, under which Germany is required to admit guilt, return the rich Alsace-Lorraine region to France, surrender its overseas colonies, and pay reparations. Under the treaty, German rearmament is strictly limited, and the Allies take temporary control of the German economy.

1920

January The League of Nations is founded to foster and maintain world peace and disarmament. The U.S. Senate rejects the treaty and America does not join the League of Nations, seriously weakening the group. It was later disbanded and replaced in 1945 by the United Nations.

CHAPTER FIVE

"OVER THERE"

The First Wave—Spring–Summer 1918

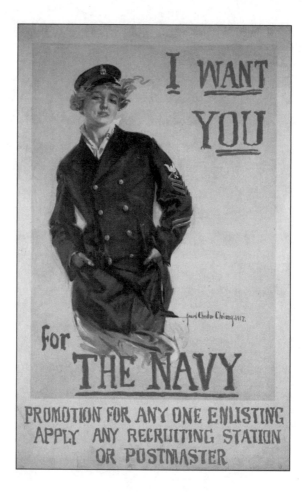

Send the word, send the word to beware,
We'll be over, we're coming over,
And we won't come back till it's over over there.
—George M. Cohan, "Over There," 1917

F OR CENTURIES FRANCE, and Paris in particular, has inspired writers, poets, painters, and composers who praised the romance of the "City of Light" and the French countryside. But in the spring of 1918, there was little beauty to celebrate in war-torn France.

Near the end of March 1918, the Germans had launched a fresh offensive against the British and French at the Somme River, scene of the war's deadliest battle in 1916. Firing mustard, chlorine, and tear gas and millions of artillery shells in the early hours of March 21, the Germans again inflicted massive casualties. It was the heaviest bombardment the British army had ever experienced. The sound of artillery could be heard across the English Channel. In late March, Paris also came under bombardment from special guns mounted on railroad cars some seventy miles away.

A 1917 navy recruiting poster by Howard Christy Chandler was supposed to make enlisting seem exciting and romantic, especially to young American men. *[Library of Congress]*

Soon all of these armies faced another threat. That spring, the storm of influenza began washing over the troops. In emergency hospitals, French soldiers were burning up with extremely high temperatures. The kaiser's soldiers were hit in April and were flattened by what they called Flanders fever.

Where had it come from? The connection had not yet been made, but the answer should have been obvious. Brest was the deep-water port where the first troops of the American Expeditionary Forces had landed. By May 1918, one million American soldiers had landed in France, many arriving at Brest. During the Atlantic crossing in March 1918, some of those troops had already been hit by flu and pneumonia. Arriving in France at the rate of some hundred thousand a month, they brought hope to their besieged French and British allies. But they also brought illness.

In early May, one division of Americans sent to the front was blitzed by the "three-day fever" even as they were attacked by German gas shells. Highly contagious, the sickness affected up to 90 percent of the men in the trenches and was quickly passed from one army to the next. From France, it rolled over the Alps and Pyrenees into Italy and Spain.

This had been the great fear of doctors like Army Surgeon General Gorgas and other medical men who knew that disease was far more deadly than war for battlefield troops. When America declared war in April 1917, Gorgas led the effort to stockpile vaccines, antitoxins, and other medicines. From long experience, Gorgas knew the risks of contagion among troops in close quarters and unsanitary conditions. He also knew better than most a historical truth: killer epidemics have been far more responsible for molding many of civilization's most significant moments than schoolbooks and some historians recognize.

"Because diseases have been the biggest killers of people, they have also been decisive shapers of history," scientist and author Jared Diamond writes in *Guns, Germs, and Steel*. "All those military histories glorifying great generals over-simplify the ego-deflating truth: the winners of past wars were not always the armies with the best generals and weapons, but were often merely those bearing the nastiest germs to transmit to their enemies."

During America's brief war with Spain that began in 1898, for instance, many more soldiers died of disease than in combat while fighting in Cuba. Thousands died from dysentery, malaria, typhoid, and the dreaded yellow fever—what soldiers called Yellow Jack. When the war ended, the U.S. Army set up boards on typhoid, tropical diseases, and yellow fever to investigate, control, and cure the deadly scourges.

Leading the commission was Dr. Walter Reed, a career army doctor who was known as one of the leading experts on diseases. The other men on the yellow fever commission were

Yellow fever was depicted as the deadly "Yellow Jack."
[Frank Leslie's Illustrated Newspaper]

U.S. Army surgeon Aristide Agramonte; Dr. James Carroll, Reed's research assistant; and Dr. Jesse W. Lazear. While the commission looked for other causes of disease—such as the possibility that disease was spread by infected bedding and clothing—they were investigating the theory that yellow fever was passed on by disease-carrying mosquitoes. It was a connection first suggested by Cuban scientist Carlos J. Finlay in 1881 but was largely dismissed and ridiculed by many other doctors, politicians, and newspapers of the day.

Jesse W. Lazear circa 1900.
[Philip S. Hench Walter Reed Yellow Fever Collection, 1806–1995. Historical Collections, Claude Moore Health Sciences Library, University of Virginia]

Working in Havana, Cuba, Dr. Carroll purposely let an infected mosquito bite him. He fell ill with yellow fever but survived. A few weeks later, Dr. Lazear also allowed himself to be bitten by a stray mosquito that had landed on him while tending patients in a yellow fever ward. He did nothing as he watched the insect take his blood. Without telling his colleagues, Lazear had apparently experimented on himself, describing an experiment on "guinea pig number 1" in his notebook.

Dr. Lazear—who had left a wife and two young children to come to Cuba—soon fell ill with an extremely violent case of yellow fever. In his final delirium, it took two men to hold Lazear down. He died on September 25, 1900, at age 34.

Convinced by Lazear's death, the yellow fever board kicked into high gear. To eradicate Havana's mosquitoes, the U.S. Army began ridding the city of mosquito-breeding sites—typically any places where water collects and is left standing. Using improved sanitation, fumigation with insecticides, and draining the wet areas where mosquitoes bred, the effort dramatically lowered the number of yellow fever cases. The dreaded Yellow Jack was virtually eliminated in the city in a matter of months.

But the press, public, and many doctors and scientists remained skeptical. Typical of the refusal to believe that insects, not bad air, caused disease was a November 1900 *Washington Post* editorial: "Of all the silly and nonsensical rigmarole of yellow fever that has yet found its way into print—and there has been enough of that to build a fleet—the silliest beyond compare is to be found in the arguments and theories generated by a mosquito hypothesis."

Although still somewhat doubtful of the mosquito theory, Dr. William Gorgas had led that cleanup effort and become a believer when he saw Havana's yellow fever cases drop to zero. Gorgas later put that Cuban experience to good use when he was assigned to rid the Panama Canal zone of yellow fever, which was slowing work on the colossal project to unite the Atlantic and Pacific Oceans. America had taken over the construction of the massive Panama Canal in 1904, but yellow fever among the workforce crippled progress. Led by Gorgas, another antimosquito campaign was launched, and while it did not eliminate yellow fever entirely in Panama, it successfully reduced the incidence of disease enough to complete the Panama Canal. (An overview of medical history can be found in Appendix I.)

One of the greatest engineering and construction feats in history, this Path Between the Seas was officially scheduled to open with a grand ceremony on August 15, 1914. But the celebrations were put on hold, and America's president, Woodrow Wilson, canceled his plans to attend. Just days before the canal

Major General William C. Gorgas, Surgeon General of the U.S. Army during World War I. [Wikimedia]

was ready for its debut, all of Europe exploded in the opening salvoes of the Great War.

As the chief medical officer of a wartime army, Gorgas was going to do everything possible to ensure the health of America's military. He had railroad cars transformed into rolling laboratories with the support of two charitable organizations, the Rockefeller Institute and the Red Cross. Gorgas had also gathered a group of world-renowned scientists to continue research and development into ways to prevent the spread of infectious diseases. A vaccine for pneumonia was at the top of their to-do list.

Like many illnesses, pneumonia triggers the immune system, the human body's highly evolved set of defenses against invasion by a host of threats. Beginning with the layer of skin that covers the body, those defenses include a simple sneeze or cough as part of their many ways to fight off invading attackers, infections, and other threats. It is, as John M. Barry explains, "an extraordinarily complex, intricate, and interwoven combination of various kinds of white blood cells, antibodies, enzymes, toxins, and other proteins. The key to the immune system is its ability to distinguish what belongs in the body, 'self,' from what does not belong, 'nonself.'"

By 1918, a generation of medical miracles had emerged from the scientific revolution of germ theory. (See Appendix I.)

Pioneers such as Robert Koch and Louis Pasteur had led the way to a variety of vaccines to battle cholera, anthrax, rabies, and a host of other diseases. But there was not yet a vaccine or other chemical compound devised to battle influenza and pneumonia. Described as "the captain of the men of death" by a prominent researcher, pneumonia was a leading cause of death around the world for years before the Spanish flu took its toll. When microbes invade the lungs, the body's immune system responds with inflammation and fluid buildup.

This building housed sick and dying soldiers at Camp Funston.
[Fort Riley Museum]

Pneumonia can kill because the fluid interferes with the lungs' essential job—transferring oxygen into the bloodstream. The microbes themselves can also move from the lungs into the bloodstream, spreading infection throughout the body.

In March 1918, influenza and pneumonia deaths at Camp Funston were growing. Besides the soldiers, the victims now included civilians. An eighteen-year-old worker in the camp's laundry when the flu struck, Jessie Lee Brown Foveaux said of her civilian coworkers, "We lost lots of them. They came in so fast and furious. We'd be working with someone one day, and they'd go home because they didn't feel good, and by the next day they were gone. Every day we wondered who was going to be next."

While the death rate at Camp Funston was high, it was not unusual enough to set off serious alarm bells—except to one man. The deadly outbreak of disease at the Kansas army camp had come a few weeks after a country doctor named Loring Miner began to take note of a particularly nasty flu "bug" spreading through rural Haskell County, Kansas.

In the first two months of 1918, Dr. Miner had been seeing a lot of flu. One local newspaper had reported in February 1918, "Most everybody over the country is having lagrippe or pneumonia." That was not uncommon. Flu season typically begins in the late fall, runs through winter, and ends in the late spring. But after some of his patients died, Dr. Miner began to make a record of what he considered an unusually severe flu—including the odd fact that otherwise healthy young men were dying. Some of these patients were falling, according to John M. Barry, "as suddenly as if they had been shot."

Even in remote Haskell County, where some farmers still lived in the sod houses first built by nineteenth-century pioneers, Dr. Miner prided himself on keeping up with the latest developments in medicine. A scientific man, he had built his own laboratory.

And he knew something was off. Dr. Miner understood healthy young men didn't typically die from a simple bout of the flu. Wondering why they couldn't fight it, he began to collect samples of blood, urine, and sputum—the saliva and mucus coughed up from the lungs. Even when the local outbreak of flu eventually ended in Haskell County, Dr. Miner was still worried. People traveling through that area could have easily picked up the illness and become contagious, carrying this flu wherever they went.

Dr. Miner's worst fear was on target. Some of the recruits who had passed through Haskell County were heading for Camp Funston. Although it is not certain that someone from Haskell County brought the influenza virus to Camp Funston, the likelihood is very strong.

"The timing of the Funston explosion," writes medical historian John M. Barry, "strongly suggests that the influenza outbreak there came from Haskell; if Haskell was the source, whoever carried it to Funston brought a mild version of the virus, but it was a virus capable of mutating back to lethality."

Public Health Service officers inspect immigrants at Ellis Island.
[Centers for Disease Control]

Dr. Miner reported his concerns to the U.S. Public Health Service, but his reports were largely ignored. At the time, there was no official mandate to report flu cases—a practice required in the United States only later, after the second wave of flu hit even harder in September 1918. Dr. Miner was writing about a fairly small outbreak in remote, isolated Kansas farm country. Public Health Service doctors were understandably in the dark. They had no way to put together pieces of the puzzle since they didn't have all the pieces. They did not know, for example, that large numbers of workers had reported sick at the Ford Motor Company in Detroit. Or that a few weeks later in April and May, nearly a quarter of the prisoners at California's San Quentin prison would fall ill.

The Public Health Service had been born in the nation's early years as the U.S. Marine Hospital Service. Its doctors were responsible for taking care of sick sailors returning to the United States and protecting the country against infectious diseases. Renamed the Public Health Service in 1912, the organization was also in charge of guarding against any illness brought into America by arriving immigrants.

By 1918, the Public Health Service was far more concerned with getting the nation's medical community ready for war. Millions of American soldiers would soon be shipped overseas to Europe's killing fields. When the United States entered the war, it had a total of 140,000 doctors, and only 776 were in the

Woman's Committee of the Council of National Defense
poster. [Library of Congress]

military. The harsh realities of war meant that hundreds of thousands of doctors would need to be trained in order to tend to the sick and wounded. The Public Health Service would be responsible in part for ensuring the education and supply of doctors.

With World War I bringing such horrible combat injuries and flu cases, the demand for trained nurses would also increase. When the war began, there were 403 women on active duty in the Army Nurse Corps, founded in 1901. By war's end, 21,480 nurses had enlisted, and over 10,000 had served overseas. The first military nurses had arrived in Europe before the first soldiers. More than two hundred died in military service, many of those from the Spanish flu.

NOT LONG AFTER Camp Funston was hit, other army and navy bases began to struggle under a growing crush of flu and pneumonia cases. A medical emergency was blossoming, but the army had a war to fight. The generals were more concerned with getting the troops combat ready and loaded onto transports.

Two months after massive numbers of Americans began arriving in France, the flu was spreading across the continent. At the end of May it appeared "with great violence" in the British Second Army. "A brigade of artillery had one third of its whole strength taken ill within forty-eight hours, and in the brigade ammunition column, only fifteen men were available for duty one day out of a strength of 145." In June, three thousand men of the British First Army were hospitalized in three days with what the medics called "P.U.O.," pyrexia (or fever) of unknown origin. By the early summer of 1918, more than two hundred thousand British soldiers in France had been taken out of service—down with the flu.

On the opposing side, the outbreak of flu was also taking a toll, with serious consequences for the kaiser's beleaguered forces. Hundreds of thousands of German troops were on sick lists with the Spanish flu. It was certainly no better for German civilians. By June 1918, the flu had become a full-fledged epidemic in Germany, where shortages caused by blockades and a decline in farm production caused by the war weakened and demoralized the German people. Where generals and tanks had failed, the Spanish flu prevailed.

And it moved around the world. The illness landed in India in late May. In Mumbai, then known as Bombay, dockworkers unloading ships were hit first. From there, the flu rode the rails, reaching Calcutta, Madras, and Rangoon, in what was then called Burma. By the end of May, China was engulfed. The flu hit New Zealand next—most likely carried around the globe by troops and cargo ships carrying supplies.

In crowded infirmaries around the world, bewildered doctors were caught off guard. The symptoms didn't fit with any known illnesses. Confronted with a patient in a London hospital, the personal physician to King George V watched a delirious soldier take deep, painful gasps of air. The young man's skin was blue, and he had raised purple blisters on his face and chest. The king's doctor said, "I fail to see any explanation."

A German military doctor was similarly perplexed. Leafing through his medical texts, he found nothing to match the raging fevers and delirium. All he could do was try to make his patients comfortable.

The facts were harsh, and there was little relief. Although a new age of wonder drugs had dawned since the late nineteenth century, the typical doctor's bag of the day contained relatively few drugs, most of them plant based. These included quinine, a malaria treatment made from the

Paul Ehrlich pioneered the concept of "magic bullets"—chemical compounds that could prevent or treat microbial diseases without harming the patient, the forerunner of modern antibiotics and chemotherapy. [Wikimedia]

bark of a tree; digitalis, which quickens the heartbeat and comes from the foxglove plant; and morphine and other pain killers derived from the opium poppy. In 1899, the German chemical company Bayer introduced aspirin, a pain reliever and fever reducer called the "miracle drug of the century." Aspirin was based on old medicinal plant remedies—bark of the willow and meadowsweet. But it was no cure for the flu.

In 1910, German scientist and physician Paul Ehrlich discovered what he called a "magic bullet"—something that could kill a disease or microorganism without killing the patient. Based on arsenic, an otherwise lethal poison, Ehrlich's salvarsan cured syphilis, a major killer of the day. But it did nothing for the flu.

Apart from the handful of vaccines, morphine and other opium-derived painkillers, aspirin tablets, Ehrlich's syphilis treatment, and a whiskey flask, the early twentieth-century medicine cabinet was pretty bare. Antibiotics—chemicals that can prevent or treat bacterial infections—would not be produced until the 1930s, and in any case, they would have had no effect on the virus that caused Spanish flu.

Even as doctors around the world struggled to identify and treat this strange and unrecognizable new disease, it seemed to disappear. The illness had moved swiftly, but by midsummer, it was fading—typical of flu season. But it wasn't gone for good.

"It had only gone underground," says John M. Barry. "Like a forest fire left burning in the roots, swarming and mutating . . . watching and waiting, waiting to burst into flame."

CHAPTER SIX

"OBEY THE LAWS

AND WEAR THE GAUZE"

The Second Wave—Autumn 1918

Obey the laws
And wear the gauze
Protect your jaws
From Septic Paws
—Public health rhyme encouraging mask use

KATHERINE PORTER was eager to get into uniform—just like Walt Disney, Franklin D. Roosevelt, and many other Americans. But for her, it would mean the crisp white dress and nursing cap emblazoned with the Red Cross symbol. A transplant from rural Texas, the twenty-eight-year-old

A streetcar in Seattle carries a warning about spitting.
[National Archives and Records Administration]

journalist was working as a reporter at Denver's *Rocky Mountain News* in the autumn of 1918. Her reviews of local events were popular with readers, and her colleagues admired Porter's knack for dashing off a newspaper column with ease and style. But as she watched young men enlist and head off to fight, she wanted to trade in her typewriter. Katherine Porter wanted to do her part.

She had already survived a bout of tuberculosis, then a deadly disease. But now Katherine was completely recovered. As anti-German propaganda filled the air in 1918 and war fever spread around the country, she set out to join the Red Cross.

The Red Cross was formed in Switzerland in 1863 as the International Committee for Relief to the Wounded. Its creation led to the first Geneva Convention in 1864, which provided for the care of injured soldiers and protected medical workers as neutral for the first time in the history of warfare. Under the terms of the convention, medical workers who wore a red cross on a white background—the inverse of the Swiss flag—were supposed to be safe from attack as they tended the wounded. The symbol became an icon. In May 1881, Clara Barton, who gained fame as a nurse during the American Civil War, launched the American branch of the Red Cross.

A private organization officially chartered by Congress to serve the nation in emergencies, the Red Cross had practically

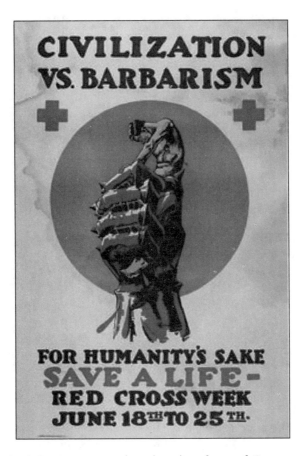

Red Cross posters also played on fears of German savagery to both recruit volunteers and raise funds for the organization. [Library of Congress]

grown into an arm of the government. With the coming of the war in Europe, the Red Cross had expanded aggressively, organizing fifty base hospitals in France and training nurses for the U.S. Army and Navy. According to Red Cross records,

Red Cross promotional posters depicted its nurses as angels
of mercy who could fix things with a smile while wearing a
crisp white blouse. *[Library of Congress]*

more than twenty-three thousand Red Cross nurses enrolled
during the war. Of these, nearly twenty thousand were assigned to active duty with the army, navy, U.S. Public Health
Service, and the Red Cross overseas.

But before she could put on a Red Cross nurse's uniform,

Katherine fell sick in October 1918. For days, she lay in bed with a dangerously high fever, her body wracked with agonizing pain. Katherine's landlady tried to put the desperately sick reporter out of the house, terrified that she would infect other

The U.S. Treasury offered inexpensive stamps as a form of war bond, saying, "Your country needs every penny which every man, woman, and child can save and loan." [Library of Congress]

boarders. The Spanish flu had hit Denver hard, and the hospitals were all full. For a time, there was no room for Katherine.

Burning with fever, Katherine was finally admitted. But it seemed to be too late. Drifting in and out of consciousness, she lay in bed with a temperature that rose to 105 degrees and remained there for days. Lingering near death, Katherine was screened off from other patients. Fellow reporters prepared her obituary. Family members made arrangements to collect her remains to be returned to Texas for burial.

As she lay dying in a hospital corridor, Katherine's chances for recovery seemed bleak. Then fate intervened. A group of young interns decided to give Katherine an experimental shot of strychnine—a deadly poison now mostly used for killing rodents. At the time, doctors tried it in very small doses as a "convulsant," to produce muscle contractions. Some athletes, including Olympic marathoners, also used injections of strychnine—what today would be called a "performance-enhancing drug."

"Miraculously, it worked," writes her biographer, Joan Givner, "and she began to fight her way back to life."

Katherine Anne Porter's fever broke. She recovered and lived. She had lost all her hair, but she was among the lucky ones.

A little more than twenty years later—in 1939—Porter published a collection of short stories called *Pale Horse, Pale*

Rider. The title story told of Miranda, a young newspaper writer in Denver who nearly dies of influenza. A gallant young beau named Adam cares for Miranda, then visits her in the hospital while home from an army training camp. Adam is not so lucky. He also comes down with the Spanish flu, but unlike Miranda and Katherine Porter, he does not survive.

In parts dreamlike, Porter's autobiographical story captured the almost surreal experience of falling victim to the Spanish flu. Many survivors reported a hazy mental state as high fever altered their perceptions of reality. The same story depicted another reality—the nation's fevered wartime mood, as Americans were urged and later pressured to buy Liberty Bonds to pay for the cost of America's involvement in World War I. In the story, two unrelenting war bond salesmen come to Miranda's office and put on a hard sell.

"The two men slid off the desk, leaving some of her papers rumpled, and the oldish man had inquired why she had not bought a Liberty Bond.... 'Look here,' he asked her, 'do you know there's a war, or don't you?'"

As her fellow workers look on, the men expect Miranda to turn over a portion of her meager salary to buy a bond.

In fact, such men were part of a force of seventy-five thousand Four Minute Men, who traveled the country giving brief speeches—the length of time it took a projectionist to change reels on a movie projector—pressing audiences at motion picture theaters, religious meetings, union meetings, and town halls to buy bonds and war savings stamps. The refusal to buy bonds meant being labeled someone who wasn't "doing their part."

The Four Minute Men were part of a larger government agency called the Committee on Public Information. Established by executive order after war was declared, the committee's purpose was to create enthusiasm and boost public support for the war effort. Although the committee's leader, George Creel, rejected the word "propaganda," that is essentially what the agency did with newsprint, posters, and eventually radio and original movies. "Liberty Sings," weekly community events where patriotic songs were sung by church choirs and barbershop quartets, were sponsored across the country. What began as a morale-building effort rapidly became a high-pressure loyalty test.

The Committee on Public Information was operating even before the United States passed a new Sedition Act, which made it a crime to "utter, print, write or publish any disloyal, profane, scurrilous, or abusive language about the form of government of the United States." A volunteer group called the American Protective League was formed and given powers by the Justice Department to enforce the Sedition Act.

Porter's fictional Miranda knew that to challenge the Committee or its Four Minute Men was no small matter. Americans were being told that refusing to support the war bond effort was one step away from treason. A poster produced by the committee left no doubt about those who did not do their part. "I am Public Opinion. All men fear me!... If you have the money to buy and do not buy, I will make this No Man's Land for you!"

Part of the propaganda effort was aimed at German Americans, who were increasingly viewed with suspicion. Some states outlawed teaching German. Famous conductor Leopold Stokowski wrote to President Wilson asking if Bach and Beethoven—both German composers—should be eliminated from his concerts. Otto Kahn, chairman of New York's Metropolitan Opera, made a similar query, asking the president if German operas and opera singers should continue at the opera house. "Wilson hated to see the loss of German opera," notes biographer A. Scott Berg, "but left the decision to Kahn and his board—which chose to bar German works."

Hamburgers were renamed "liberty steaks" and sauerkraut was called "liberty cabbage." Berlin, Iowa, changed its name to Lincoln, and Brooklyn's Hamburg Street was renamed Wilson. Even beer was suspect. According to Alfred W. Crosby, "American brewers, condemned because of their Teutonic names and the Germanness of beer and ale," had to defend their loyalty with a newspaper ad.

The anti-German mood of the country—similar to the

anti-Irish Catholic intolerance of an earlier age and the anti-Muslim fervor of post-9/11 America—was pushed by propaganda that depicted all Germans as untrustworthy and dangerous.

Against this atmosphere of supposed German spies and saboteurs—and the spreading flu epidemic—there was no letup in the push to sell war bonds. On September 28, 1918, the nationwide frenzy to support the war bond campaign was on full display when Philadelphia's leaders pressed on with their Liberty Loan parade, intended to sell millions of dollars' worth of war bonds. Philadelphia was a major port city and shipbuilding site, situated between two major army bases—Camp Dix in New Jersey and Camp Meade in Maryland. The organizers hoped to stage the greatest parade in the city's history, with thousands marching and a huge crowd lining the streets to watch.

While some physicians counseled caution, money spoke louder. Fear of spreading contagion took a back seat to a distorted sense of civic-mindedness as Philadelphia health officials assured the public that they would be safe—the military would contain the illness. These officials seemed more concerned with getting out big crowds and meeting bond quotas.

False hope and wishful thinking also kicked in. Optimistic reports—later proven wrong—suggested that the flu had already disappeared among the Allied troops in Europe. Hopes flew even higher when the *Philadelphia Inquirer* reported that a researcher had found the likely cause of the flu—a bacteria called Pfeiffer's bacillus, named after the nineteenth-century German scientist who had discovered it. But it was a case of mistaken identity. The public had also been told with confidence that a vaccine might soon be ready. That, too, was wrong.

Deciding that the show must go on, the city health commissioner approved the march. Filled with bands, Boy Scouts, marines, and sailors, the line of marchers stretched for two miles. More than two hundred thousand massed on the sidewalks on September 28.

Soon after the parade ended, the floodgates opened. In just two days, some 635 cases of influenza were reported. Short-staffed hospitals quickly filled to capacity and the health commissioner declared an epidemic existed. Schools were ordered closed, along with all places of "public amusement," including theaters and bowling alleys. Some wary members of the press, thinking that the city was overreacting, condemned the closings as a violation of common sense and personal freedom.

The flu hit shortly after Frank Biberstein started school at St. Joseph's College and Seminary in Philadelphia. He and other seminary students were put to work, walking the streets with a horse-drawn cart to collect the dead. They went door to door, calling for victims. Once they retrieved a few bodies, they would return to a makeshift field hospital. Decades later Frank

Biberstein would tell his family tales of bringing out the dead, much as it had been done in medieval Europe in the days of the Black Death.

"They would do this for several hours a day and he did it for most of the semester," his grandson Paul Kendall relates. "My grandfather was not a big man, so I remember him telling me how hard it was for him to carry the bodies out. He said there was no one else who would or could collect the dead, so the powers-that-be decided that they would get the young men studying to be religious to do the work."

Also filling the void was Philadelphia's well-organized Visiting Nurses. These women worked around the clock, assisting those who were sick but unable to get to a hospital. They often entered houses to find starving orphaned children, alone beside the corpses of their dead parents.

"Visiting nurses often walked into scenes resembling those of the plague years of the fourteenth century," historian Alfred Crosby notes. "They drew crowds of supplicants—or people shunned them for fear of the white gauze masks that they often wore. They could go out in the morning with a list of fifteen patients to see and end up seeing fifty. One nurse found a husband dead in the same room where his wife lay with newly born twins. It had been twenty-four hours since the death and the births, and the wife had no food but an apple which happened to be within reach."

A public health nurse teaches a young mother how to sterilize a
bottle. *[National Library of Medicine]*

Just as plague had transformed medieval daily life during
the Black Death, the Spanish flu was changing America—and
rarely for the best. The crisis was producing acts of courage,
but also cowardice. While many communities saw armies of
volunteers willing to risk their own health to help the sick,
there were also many people who turned their backs, too
frightened to go to the aid of infected friends or family.

As a young girl, Mary McCarthy had witnessed this fearful mood during the fatal weeks after the epidemic struck her birthplace of Seattle, Washington. McCarthy would later describe a time "when no hospital beds were to be had and people went about with masks or stayed shut up in their houses, and the awful fear of contagion paralyzed all services and made each man an enemy to his neighbor."

McCarthy's parents left Seattle to take shelter with family members in Minneapolis after the flu hit Seattle. "We began to be sure it was all an adventure," she later remembered of the train trip halfway across the country. Then both of her parents fell ill, and her mother raised suspicions as she lay listless in the sleeping berth while the train rolled east. "We saw our father draw a revolver on the conductor who was trying to put us off the train at a small wooden station in the middle of the North Dakota prairie."

After both her parents died, Mary McCarthy and her brothers were turned over to an aunt and uncle who were harsh and abusive. In a 1957 memoir, *Memories of a Catholic Girlhood*, she described the loss that she and her brothers had suffered. "We were beaten all the time, as a matter of course, with the hairbrush across the legs for ordinary occasions, and with the razor strop across the bare bottom for special occasions. . . . It was as though these ignorant people, at sea with four frightened children, had taken a Dickens novel—*Oliver Twist*, perhaps or *Nicholas Nickleby*—for a navigation chart."

Mary McCarthy and her brothers were part of a flood of broken homes and orphaned children left across the country in the flu's wake. The health commissioner of New York estimated that twenty-one thousand children had been orphaned in the city. A small town in New Hampshire counted twenty-four orphans, and in a Pennsylvania coal town with a population of six thousand, some two hundred children were orphaned. Many of these children became premature adults, forced to fend for themselves by heading to work in factories. Some wound up in Dickensian "orphan asylums." Many others, like Mary McCarthy and her brothers, were taken in by extended family—not always with happy results.

Even the loss of one parent could have life-changing consequences. "For Lillian Kancianich, who was born just a few months before the epidemic in 1918, her mother's death meant the break-up of her home," records historian Nancy K. Bristow, "because local custom discouraged older men from living without a woman in a household with children." According to Bristow, children were displaced even while a father survived, and some, like Lillian, were shuffled from place to place. "No one adopted me," Lillian later told Bristow. "I just went from home to home.... I had six different homes." The flu epidemic and her mother's death, Bristow says, changed Lillian's life completely.

All innocence was lost for children who had to play a new role, some taking jobs to support their orphaned siblings. Children as young as ten years old were called on to work as "runners"—doing errands and carrying home pails of food for sick adults. In many places, children became accustomed to seeing the unthinkable. The sight of entire families dead in their yards became as common as going out to play. It is worth remembering, however, that working children were not un-usual in early-twentieth-century America, before federal child labor laws were passed. While some states had begun to limit child labor, many children worked in mines, textile factories, and cotton fields, selling newspapers, and shining shoes.

All of this was taking place in a very different America. In the early twentieth century, the federal government provided few of the resources that are commonplace today. There was no Social Security, federal welfare assistance, unemployment, or disability insurance. Modern medical assistance programs— such as Medicare for senior citizens and Medicaid for those in poverty—did not exist. Neither did agencies like FEMA, the Federal Emergency Management Agency, which coordinates disaster response today.

When the Spanish flu pandemic hit Massachusetts, Lieu-tenant Governor Calvin Coolidge—a future U.S. president—

In 1916, Lewis Hine documented five-year-old Mart Payne picking cotton. This photograph was part of a series that Hine took while working as an investigative photographer for the National Child Labor Committee.

[Library of Congress]

wired Washington for help. The hard-hit state was home to Camp Devens and Boston, and it desperately needed doctors. With Americans now fully engaged in combat in France creating a pressing need for military doctors and nurses, there were precious few to spare. Other than producing posters and informational pamphlets of dubious value, the federal government was channeling most of its energy and efforts into the war. "If influenza could have been smothered by paper," says historian Alfred Crosby, "many lives could have been saved in 1918."

The best Congress could do was authorize an emergency fund of one million dollars—a substantial amount of money, but far from enough for the crisis the country faced. This meant that many local communities across America had to fend for themselves, especially African Americans. They often had to cope with even less assistance from federal, state, and local governments, and the broader white world. In 1918, America was still living through its Jim Crow era of sharp racial segregation—and not just in the southern states of the former Confederacy. Philadelphia had one of the largest black communities in America at the time, but the city's hospitals were segregated. In Philadelphia and elsewhere, hospitals that accepted black patients usually assigned them to separate wards, often shamefully located in attics or unheated basements.

"Racism and legalized segregation restricted access by

black patients and health professionals to health-care facilities," physician and medical historian Vanessa Northington Gamble writes. "In addition, African Americans lacked political and economic power and lived in the least desirable and most disease-ridden neighborhoods. But despite their plight, African Americans created separate hospitals, facilities, and organizations to take care of themselves. During the 1918 influenza epidemic, these institutions proved essential because of rigid racial barriers in medicine and public health."

In Philadelphia, there were two black hospitals. One of them, the Frederick Douglass Memorial Hospital, quickly filled its seventy-five beds. An emergency annex was established in a nearby black parochial school. The facility operated without support from the city's political or health officials.

In part because of deep-seated racism and institutional segregation, statistics about the Spanish flu's impact on African Americans as a whole are incomplete. Anecdotal evidence and insurance company records suggest that African American communities were not hit as hard as some white areas, even in the same cities. It may have been that some black neighborhoods had absorbed the first wave of the milder Spanish flu and, as a consequence, developed greater immunity when the second wave hit. There is also the possibility that segregation— being physically separated from the white world—may have provided some protection, a kind of unintended quarantine.

Jim Crow attitudes divided the medical world as well. When the United States entered the war, the army did not accept black nurses. The war and the flu created a new reality, according to Gamble. "The influenza epidemic did what the war could not—it forced the Army to drop its ban on black nurses. On December 1, 1918, three weeks after the war ended, 18 black nurses arrived in Ohio at Camps Sherman and Grant, where large numbers of black soldiers were stationed. Although the nurses lived in segregated quarters, they took care of black and white soldiers."

Those nurses, doing their duty in the face of racism, were one example of the often selfless dedication of those who took care of the sick and dying. The Spanish flu made heroes of countless everyday people, many of whom volunteered long hours, whether it was tending victims or rolling Red Cross bandages.

But as in almost every catastrophe, others saw opportunity in tragedy—a chance to make a quick dollar and profit from a crisis. Price gouging became commonplace for everything from groceries to funerals. In Philadelphia, some undertakers raised their prices by more than 500 percent as grieving families sought proper burials. Tales spread throughout the city of individuals being forced to pay as much as fifteen dollars—a significant amount of money in 1918, especially for the poor—to dig graves for dead family members.

The delay in burying the unembalmed dead went beyond a question of common decency. It was a matter of public health. Rotting cadavers often led to the spread of other diseases. Philadelphia appealed to the federal government to meet its need for embalmers, and the army sent men to assist.

But the demand was overwhelming. "Wagonloads of bodies, some dead over a week, were buried" in potter's field, a public mass cemetery for the poor, Philadelphia nurse James F. Armstrong recounts in discussing the history of Philadelphia's nurses during the crisis. "Highway workers dug large trenches and filled them to capacity. The promise that bodies could later be retrieved and reinterred after the epidemic subsided persuaded relatives to give up loved ones. Relatives never recovered most of the bodies."

The most visible symbol of the pandemic in many places had become the gauze masks. Thought to be effective in slowing the spread of flu when first tried in one of the army camps, the masks were soon worn everywhere. Police officers, streetcar conductors, postal carriers, and even professional baseball players were required to wear them.

As demand for these masks grew, the Red Cross had its volunteers turn out masks instead of rolling bandages for soldiers. In time, many cities began to require their use.

In Minneapolis, for instance, directions for wearing the masks were issued to the public.

St. Louis Red Cross Motor Corps on duty. *[Library of Congress]*

The outside of a face mask is marked with a black thread woven into it. Always wear this side away from the face. Wear the mask to cover the nose and the mouth, tying two tapes around the head above the ears. Tie the other tapes

rather tightly around the neck. Never wear the mask of an-
other person. When the mask is removed . . . it should be care-
fully folded with the inside folded in, immediately boiled and
disinfected. When the mask is removed by one seeking to pro-
tect himself from the influenza it should be folded with the
inside folded out and boiled ten minutes. Persons considerably
exposed to the disease should boil their masks at least once
a day.

ONE DOCTOR on the Minnesota State Board of Health advocated wearing the masks but did not wear one himself, saying,
"I personally prefer to take my chances."

When worn by a flu victim, the mask was meant to prevent
the infectious droplets from being expelled. In San Francisco
the gauze masks were required of the entire public in a trial
ordinance, later expanded to include San Diego. In Philadelphia and other cities, this rhyme was promoted as a popular
way to remind people of the ordinance:

Obey the laws
And wear the gauze
Protect your jaws
From Septic Paws.

CHAPTER SEVEN

THE WORLD TURNED UPSIDE DOWN

*Sick with influenza? Use Ely's Cream Balm. No more
snuffling. No struggling for breath.*
—Philadelphia newspaper advertisement

THERE SEEMED TO be no end to it. As the epidemic continued its death march, and as more cities began requiring
the use of masks, it quickly became evident that they did little
good. Often used improperly, the clumsy masks were simply
not sufficient to stop or contain a microscopic virus. Many
people also failed to take proper care of the masks, which

required careful procedures to disinfect after being used. Other people simply disregarded the order.

The experimental vaccines being rushed into production were also of little or no value. As historian John M. Barry writes: "No medicine and none of the vaccines developed then could prevent influenza. . . . The virus was too efficient, too explosive, too good at what it did. In the end the virus did its will around the world."

Within weeks of the outbreak in Boston, Philadelphia, and other American cities, the Spanish flu was touching nearly every corner of the earth. A remarkable seventy-five thousand cases of flu were recorded in Odessa, the Black Sea port in the Ukraine. It moved across South America, where people dropped in the streets as they waited for streetcars.

In Cape Town, South Africa, fifteen hundred workers returned from war service aboard a cargo ship laden with dead crewmen and laborers. The ship should have been quarantined, but infected passengers got off. Cape Town witnessed scenes that might come from a zombie horror movie.

"Men and women stopped as suddenly as if stabbed," historian Richard Collier writes, "clutching desperately at lamp-posts or telegraph-poles—then slid, in agonizing slow motion, to

PRECEDING PAGES: Employees at a Seattle drug company during the 1918 pandemic [Max London, Stanford University]

collapse unconscious at the base." As volunteers strived to make soup to feed the sick, the city's butchers were down with the flu, unable to provide meat. Medical students helped out, "trading their scalpels for cleavers."

In Freetown, Sierra Leone—one of the best deep-water ports in West Africa—five hundred dockworkers came down with the flu almost immediately after a British navy ship sailed into port with two hundred sick sailors aboard. The disease spread to the general population, and an estimated two-thirds of the native population fell sick, resulting in more than one thousand deaths within a month.

A man operating a large elevator at a South African gold mine was lifting miners out of a deep mineshaft when he was suddenly overwhelmed by the flu. He lost control of the elevator, and dozens of miners plunged to their deaths. "The scourge had struck at five continents," Collier writes. "No longer was it an epidemic but a pandemic that was in force."

Anxious people tried everything—even closing windows and vents to keep out "bad air." In the stifling heat of places like the tropical island of Jamaica, that was deadly for shut-ins. Unfortunately, cutting air flow and proper ventilation was the opposite of what many doctors had discovered—fresh air was actually of great benefit, both in preventing infection and improving the chances of survival.

Many doctors also recommended alcohol—as a preventive,

a remedy, and finally, to ease the end. Bourbon and whiskey sales boomed in 1918. As army camps everywhere remained on high alert through the autumn of 1918, Clarence Crump Ross, a college graduate with hopes of becoming a doctor, was heading to medical school when he was drafted and assigned to Camp Perry in Ohio, another large cantonment filled with trainees. When the Spanish flu hit, Ross was given the assignment to "dose" the dying soldiers with whiskey he carried in a five-gallon ceramic jug. "Although he didn't drink himself," his daughter, Martha Wrigley, recalls, "after having to give a drink to so many dying soldiers, he began having a sip himself!"

But Ross had another job. Dealing with the camp casualties meant removing the dead men's dog tags—small metal tags that identify military personnel—and tying them around their right big toes. Ross's daughter reports a macabre scene of the burial detail: "One deceased soldier's body was folded at the waist when it was thrown onto the wagon. When the air in the dead man's lungs expelled, it caused him to emit a ghostly moan; the sound scared everyone near the wagon, sending them running."

IN OTHER ARMY BASES, nurses didn't even wait for death. They tagged toes while the patients were still alive, certain that most cases were hopeless.

The son of Norwegian immigrants who lived in Minnesota,

Arne Thompson served as a private in the Army Coast Artillery Corps. When the Spanish flu reached Camp Dodge, near Des Moines, Iowa, where thousands of soldiers were housed, Arne was put on a burial detail. Watching bunkmates and fellow recruits falling around him was tragic—and frightening. But he did his duty, digging graves for the stacks of bodies; seven hundred soldiers died of the flu at Camp Dodge in October 1918.

"My dad came down with the flu while performing the aforementioned duty and was deathly sick, but didn't die," writes Arne Thompson's son David. "He lived to be honorably discharged from the Army on Christmas Eve 1918. He was given $30 separation pay and a train ticket home to Paynesville, MN. . . . When I asked him, 'What did you do in World War I?' All my dad would say to me was, 'I survived the flu.'"

AS THE CRISIS WORSENED across the country and around the world, people searched frantically for remedies. Newspapers were filled with advertisements for the latest in oils, pills, drinks, and balms that promised quick relief, but few remedies made any difference. Some were dangerous. Strict quarantine, plenty of bed rest, fresh air, and "tender loving care" seemed to work best. But all were often in short supply during wartime and widespread panic.

Reflecting some of the desperation in the air, Philadelphia

newspapers, including the University of Pennsylvania's *Daily Pennsylvanian*, reported a panicked community making a frenzied run on all medical supplies. Based on published accounts from October 1918, writer Eileen Lynch recounts:

> *Frantic shoppers strip pharmacy shelves bare. The press of customers is so great that the Philadelphia College of Pharmacy and Temple University suspend classes so that pharmacy students can help fill prescriptions. Most are for whiskey, which, now that saloons are closed, is available only in drugstores. Rather than wait to become a statistic, people turn to home remedies: goose-grease poultices, sulfur fumes, onion syrup, chloride of lime.*

SNAKE-OIL ARTISTS hawked their useless potions in newspaper ads:

Use Oil of Hyomei. Bathe your breathing organs with antiseptic balsam.

Munyon's Paw Paw Pills for influenza insurance.

Sick with influenza? Use Ely's Cream Balm. No more snuffling. No struggling for breath.

DESPERATE PEOPLE turned to home remedies, trying just about anything that was rumored or advertised to stave off the flu or ease its symptoms. "Quacks and naysayers," writes medical historian Julian A. Navarro, "advocated a host of alternatives such as raw onions rubbed on the chest, creosote baths, and the consumption of large quantities of brown sugar."

It was not just a panicked public that was desperately seeking remedies. Overwhelmed army doctors, John M. Barry writes, "tried everything, everything they could think of, until they finally took

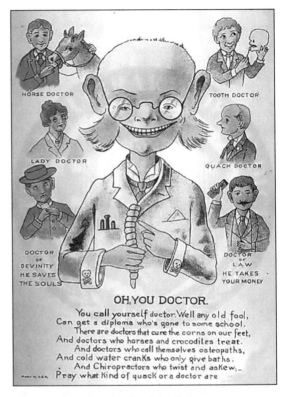

The American medical profession was very different at the beginning of the twentieth century, with less rigorous training and fewer requirements than typical today. [National Library of Medicine]

pity and stopped, abandoning some of the more brutal—and useless—treatments they had tried 'on account of [their] heroic character.' By then they had seen enough of heroism from dying soldiers."

In early November 1918, a group of sailors demonstrated a different kind of courage. Sixty-two sailors were in the navy's brig, or jail, on Deer Island, just outside Boston. The city of

Boston and nearby Camp Devens had been among the chief ignition points for the return of the pandemic in the autumn of 1918. These men had all been convicted and jailed for crimes committed while in service. Now they were being offered a deal. Would they agree to join a study of how the flu spread? In exchange for being deliberately exposed to the flu, they would receive pardons for their crimes—if they lived through it, that is.

It was an ethical bargain that left the doctor's ancient principle—"first, do no harm"—at the laboratory door. Using these jailed sailors as willing guinea pigs, the doctors surely thought, might save millions of lives. Today medical ethics consider such bargains illegal. But in 1918, as crisis raged, these ethical questions and legalities did not exist. As journalist Gina Kolata explains, "Prisoners were thought to be the ideal study subjects. They could offer up their bodies for science and, if they survived, their pardons could be justified because they gave something back to society."

Normally, such tests and studies are first performed on animals, such as lab rats or rabbits. That was the way to isolate what was causing the disease and perhaps test ways to protect humans against it. But the flu seemed to be a human disease, and the only way to test it, thought the researchers, was to give it to people. The urgency of the crisis led to drastic—and ethically questionable—measures.

To the surprise of some, all sixty-two healthy men accepted the deal. Setting to work, the navy doctors collected infectious mucus from the noses and throats of victims in the contagion ward. As gross as it sounds, this mucus was then sprayed directly into the noses and throats of the test subjects. In one case, they even injected blood from a sick man into a healthy man. They also took the healthy prisoners into the sick wards to expose them up close to flu patients.

Not a single one of these healthy test patients got the flu. Once again, the Spanish flu was confounding the scientists and raising more questions than were answered. How did the disease spread? Why did some people get sick when others did not? Could these sailors have been exposed to a mild earlier strain of the flu and developed immunity? Or, as Gina Kolata explains, "maybe those Boston sailors were the lucky ones, the people who could never become ill with flu because they had some inborn protection against the disease." Their good fortune would remain a medical mystery, but these sailors received their promised pardons.

Many of the men and women on board ships heading for Europe had no such luck. In late September 1918, Ernest W. Gibson, a company commander from Vermont, marched with his men to the *Leviathan*, the same ship on which Franklin D. Roosevelt had fallen sick. The *Leviathan* would carry them to France, but on the road a calamity was unfolding before Gibson's eyes.

"The victims of the epidemic fell on either side of the road unable to carry their heavy packs," he would recall. "Some threw their equipment away and with determination tried to keep up with their comrades. Army trucks and ambulances following picked up those who had fallen and took them back to the camp hospital. How many men and how much equipment was lost on that march has never been determined."

The situation only worsened once they were on board and bound for what Gibson called "the Great Adventure." With more than nine thousand men, along with two hundred army nurses, heading for France, the ship was an incubator of influenza. And there was no fresh air because the portholes were closed at night to keep the ship dark in case German U-boats were patrolling nearby.

"The ship was packed, conditions were such that the Influenza . . . could breed and multiply with extraordinary swiftness," said Gibson. "The number of sick increased rapidly. Washington was appraised [sic] of the situation, but the call for men for the allied armies was so great that we must go on at any cost. The sick bay became overcrowded and it became necessary to evacuate the greater portion of Deck E and turn that into sick quarters. Doctors and nurses were stricken."

The ship turned into a floating chamber of horrors. Pools

of blood that poured from the men's bleeding noses were everywhere. Attendants in bloodied shoes tracked the infected blood through the ship's narrow passages. The decks were wet with the bloody mucus and gore. Men screamed for help, until as a navy report put it, "a true inferno reigned supreme."

Lieutenant Commander Henry A. May was senior medical officer assigned to the *Leviathan* on that nightmare sailing and made an official report:

> *The conditions during this night cannot be visualized by anyone who has not actually seen them.... The nurses made a valiant effort to clean up and the navy hospital corpsmen did marvels of work, but always against tremendous odds.... Many of them worked twenty-four hours at a stretch amid conditions that can never be understood by one ashore.... Some of the embalming detail, worked at their gruesome task forty-eight hours without complaint, and at the end I had to drive them away to bath and bed.*

ONCE THE SHIP LANDED, the dying only continued. Army hospital authorities removed nearly one thousand flu and pneumonia patients from the *Leviathan*. Nearly two hundred men from Gibson's Fifty-Seventh Pioneer Infantry unit were buried in the American cemetery in Lambezellec, France, overlooking the sea near Brest.

To the influenza virus, it did not matter which side they were on.

"Following a week on the front line, we were again moved back to the resistance line, since the battalion which was to relieve us was almost wiped out by Spanish influenza," German veteran Ernst Jünger later recalled. "Several men a day reported sick in our company as well. In the division next to ours, the epidemic rages to such an extent that an enemy airman dropped leaflets promising that the British would come and relieve them, if the unit weren't withdrawn. But we learned that sickness was also spreading among the enemy; even though, we with our poor rations, were more prone to it. Young men in particular sometimes died overnight."

For Jünger and other Germans, the news was only growing worse. In August, the German army had begun to suffer mass surrenders by its soldiers who threw down their arms in the face of Allied forces. Their commander, Ludendorff, was convinced that Germany had lost the war and offered to resign. "Several hundred thousand soldiers well behind the lines either deserted or else remained in uniform but evaded orders to go to the front," Adam Hochschild writes. "In the minds of the German high command was a rising fear that, if army discipline and morale collapsed, something even worse than an Allied victory could occur: revolution at home."

By October 3, Germany was forced to form a new

government, and word was sent to President Wilson with an appeal for peace negotiations—an offer Woodrow Wilson rejected. When thousands of German sailors mutinied in early November, refusing orders to sail into battle, and revolutionaries seized the kaiser's Berlin palace, the end was near.

While the raging flu meant that there was little good news in America or much of the rest of the world, November 11 would change that. On that day, Germany accepted an armistice, or cease-fire treaty. In reality, it was a German surrender. Fighting would end at the "eleventh hour of the eleventh day of the eleventh month."

The "war to end all wars" had come to an end.

The date of November 11 would be celebrated in America as Armistice Day starting in 1919 to remember the war and the sacrifices that had been made. In 1938 Armistice Day became a national holiday, dedicated to world peace and honoring the veterans of World War I. In 1954, after the Second World War and the Korean War, Armistice Day was changed to Veterans Day and is meant to honor all American veterans.

CHAPTER EIGHT

PEACE AND PLAGUE

Normally corpses [in India] were cremated in burning ghats, level spaces at the top of the stepped riverbank, and the ashes given to the river. The supply of firewood was quickly exhausted, making cremation impossible, and the rivers became clogged with corpses.
—John M. Barry, *The Great Influenza*

HAD AN ASSASSIN poisoned the president?

It was April 3, 1919. Woodrow Wilson, the former scholar, university president, and reluctant warrior who had become America's unflinching wartime commander in chief, was in Paris. Acclaimed as a hero by much of the world, Wilson was there to negotiate a peaceful end to the dreadful conflict that had cost the world so much.

Then President Wilson got sick. Violently sick. He staggered from the room where the leaders of the victorious Allies were meeting.

"The attack was very sudden," his physician Cary T. Grayson reported a few days later. "At three o'clock he was apparently all right; at six he was seized with violent paroxysms of coughing, which were so severe and frequent that it interfered with his breathing. He had a fever of 103 and a profuse diarrhoea. I was at first suspicious that his food had been tampered with."

Wilson suffered from intense back pain and headaches, but it was not poison as his physician feared.

President Wilson had the flu. It may have been a different virus and not the more deadly Spanish flu, which had struck the White House staff in the fall of 1918. In November Wilson's influential senior adviser, Edward House, had fallen sick with Spanish flu in Paris as he laid the groundwork for the peace conference. House survived but was left seriously weakened. Three other men who were part of the American Peace Commission had also fallen victim. One of them, Willard Straight—a prominent banker, diplomat, and a founder of the *New Republic* magazine—died in Paris on December 1, 1918. While flu deaths in Paris had begun to fall from

FOLLOWING PAGES: Armistice Day—November 11, 1918: Philadelphians gather beneath a replica of the Statue of Liberty on Broad Street. *[Wikimedia]*

President Woodrow Wilson in 1919. [Library of Congress]

pandemic levels, they were still far above the normal numbers.
In February 1919, according to Alfred Crosby, the general
death rate surged. "The effect of the Spanish influenza on the
people of Paris did not fade away until spring. Such levels
of morbidity and mortality must have influenced the peace
conference."

When Wilson took ill in April, he spent four and a half

days in his sickbed, designating Edward House to take his place at the negotiations. Exasperated by the demands of the French, an exhausted Wilson threatened to leave the conference. But he rejoined the talks on April 8, even though Dr. Grayson said he was wobbly and "markedly showing the effects" of his illness. Wilson pushed through with the negotiations that secured the Treaty of Versailles, which would formally end the Great War. The president had pressed on, even while not fully recovered, said his doctor, because the stakes were so high.

Dr. Grayson wrote home from Europe, "The whole of civilization seemed to be in the balance. And without him and his guidance Europe would certainly have turned to Bolshevism and anarchy. From your side of the water you can not realize on what thin ice European civilization has been skating.... Some day perhaps I may be able to tell the world what a close call we had."

AFTER THE WAR FINALLY came to a close in November 1918, harsh reality set in for Germany's leaders and people. The once-mighty German empire had simply run out of able-bodied men to throw against the Allies. War and disease had come at a high price. "In half-starving Germany," writes World War I chronicler Adam Hochschild, "some 400,000 people had died of influenza in 1918 alone."

In late September, General Ludendorff, the German commander, had delivered the bleak truth to the kaiser. There was no longer any chance of winning the war.

Behind the lines, there was chaos. "Cold, hungry, and ragged," historian Richard Collier writes, "the people had lost all heart for war. Meatless weeks were commonplace; the bread ration had been cut, and potatoes, too. In Germany's industrial heartland, the Ruhr, the silent smokeless chimneys told their own story.... When the German armies began their great retreat from Belgium, 1000 workers had thronged the streets, outside the Reichstag [Germany's Parliament building], clamouring for peace."

By then, the kaiser—the all highest warlord—had lost the confidence of the military. Germany was about to lose its sources of oil, coal, copper, and wheat as the Allies captured its territory and German allies surrendered. Kaiser Wilhelm chose to abdicate—surrender the German imperial throne—and escape Germany.

On November 10, Wilhelm crossed the border by train and went into exile in the Netherlands, which had remained neutral throughout the war. By then, Germany's allies had begun to fall away. Bulgaria surrendered. The Turks gave in on October 30—effectively marking the end of a six-hundred-year-old Ottoman Empire. Austria-Hungary signed an agreement on November 3, as starving people rioted in the streets.

King George V of the United Kingdom later wrote that he looked on his cousin as "the greatest criminal in history." While some political leaders called for the kaiser to be arrested and hanged, President Wilson of the United States rejected this, arguing that prosecuting Wilhelm would destabilize international order and risk the chance for peace.

Securing that peace for Germany would be left at first to fifty-one-year-old Prince Max of Baden, the newly appointed chancellor of Germany. On October 22, the very day he had addressed the Reichstag to explain his plan for peace with honor, Prince Max came down with the flu. "The plague that had sapped the Kaiser's Army had cut down the Imperial Chancellor to the size of any Hindenburg Line rookie," writes historian Richard Collier. "Prince Max was luckier than he knew. Despite the raging 103° F fever that pinned him to his sick-bed, he was still in good enough physical shape to follow the daily reports."

By January 1919, the leaders of the Allies met near Paris to finalize the settlement. Three men would dominate the negotiations: President Woodrow Wilson, French Prime Minister Georges Clemenceau, and British Prime Minister David Lloyd George—who had also survived a bout of the flu. Great Britain and France, in particular, were bent on revenge and punishing Germany for the war.

French Prime Minister Clemenceau was most determined

to keep Germany weak. He wanted to make sure that Germany would never again threaten the peace of Europe. Lloyd George of Great Britain also wanted to punish Germany but without creating a new threat to stability and order. Like many leaders, he feared Russia's Bolshevik revolution might spread across Europe. President Woodrow Wilson was more conciliatory and focused on an idealistic vision of global peace under a League of Nations, a world organization that would settle differences between countries without war. In the early months of 1919, the three men argued vehemently. Several times, the negotiations almost broke down with one participant or another threatening to walk out. An agreement was finally reached in June 1919. The Germans did not have a seat at the table.

The cost of the "war to end all wars" was nightmarish—almost beyond modern understanding. Even today, the numbers of total wartime casualties are estimates. More than ten million soldiers died on the battlefields of Europe. Almost an entire generation of young men was decimated in Russia, Germany, Great Britain, and France. The Russian combat death toll was 1,811,000; 1,400,000 French soldiers died (more than 4 percent of the French population); and 908,000 British. Among Germany and its allies, more than four million soldiers died; the German dead numbered 1,800,000; Austrians, 1,200,000; and Turks, 325,000. American losses for its short-term involvement in the war were 130,174 dead and missing and more than two hundred thousand wounded.

Those were the dead fighters—another twenty million people died of hunger and other war-related causes. And countless millions had died of the Spanish flu.

Given these horrific losses, the Allies were not in a forgiving mood, and the Versailles Treaty showed that they expected Germany to pay for the war that everyone had helped to start. But far more dangerous than the impossible economic terms demanded of Germany, Austria, Hungary, and Turkey was the radical redrawing of the world map.

Through the treaty and its later multilateral agreements, Hungary, once part of a huge empire, lost two-thirds of its lands and was reduced to fewer than eight million people. The independent states of Yugoslavia, Czechoslovakia, and Poland, with a corridor to the Baltic, were arbitrarily carved out of former Austro-Hungarian and German territory. Almost three million Austro-Germans were incorporated into Czechoslovakia. They were known as Sudeten Germans, and that name would loom large a few years later when a rebuilt Germany led by Adolf Hitler marched into the Sudetenland. The other half of the former empire became tiny Austria. And in 1939, it, too, would become part of the rationale for Nazi Germany's aggression.

The lands of the Middle East that had been the Ottoman

Empire were split among the winners, leaving Turkey a small, impoverished state. The Balkan Peninsula, part of the Ottoman Empire, was divided into a handful of new states, including Czechoslovakia and Yugoslavia.

The British took Palestine, Jordan, and oil-rich Mesopotamia (modern Iraq). France won Lebanon and Syria while expanding its holdings in French Indochina—including what is now Vietnam. A young Vietnamese student who had been living in Paris where he worked as a kitchen assistant at the Ritz hotel attempted to get independent status for his country. "Ho Chi Minh—and Vietnam—were too obscure even to receive an answer," writes Margaret MacMillan in a history of the Paris 1919 negotiations. Minh later went to Moscow to study the revolutionary techniques that he would eventually use to wrest Vietnam away from the French and American armies. The German possessions in Africa and the Pacific were similarly divided among the victors under a League of Nations mandate that simply transferred control of these African lands to new colonial powers.

In all these postwar dealings, something else was at stake: the future of Europe and the world. The seeds were being sown for the next war in Europe as well as generations of deadly division in the Middle East, Africa, Eastern Europe, and Indochina. And men of the time knew it. Lloyd George of

Great Britain even predicted, "We shall have to fight another war all over again in twenty-five years."

Most historians acknowledge that the British prime minister's 1919 prediction was tragically accurate. He was off by just a few years. Europe went to war again in September 1939—an even more devastating conflict that grew into World War II.

The terms of the Versailles Treaty trouble historians. Many of the toughest and most punishing French demands—forcing Germany to accept responsibility, surrendering territory, stripping its colonies away, imposing strict limits on its military forces, heavy war reparations (payments to the victorious allies for the cost of the war) were approved under the final terms.

Wilson's illness had clearly complicated the situation, making it difficult for him to participate in key negotiations during the conference. "He was not physically or mentally the man he had been," comments Margaret MacMillan. "He never effectively functioned as president again, although he continued to influence the battle over the treaty from his sickroom."

The resulting treaty was significantly different from the one Wilson had wanted when he sailed for France. Witnesses and observers in Paris, including Wilson's advisers and personal doctor, were concerned about his state of mind and strength as the negotiations wore on. Weakened by the flu, or even impaired by it in some way, Wilson clearly abandoned some of his principles at Versailles—particularly on the issue of German reparations. Describing the American president at the time as "the pathetic, broken Wilson," Margaret MacMillan writes that he "betrayed his own principles, his country and the hopes of all who wanted a better world."

Did his bout of flu—if it was in fact the flu—change history?

Wilson biographer A. Scott Berg writes, "In April 1919, at the moment of physical and nervous exhaustion, Woodrow Wilson was struck by a viral infection that had neurological ramifications. . . . Generally predictable in his actions, Wilson began blurting unexpected orders. . . . He sometimes stopped speaking because he had convinced himself that all

The war was over, but the Spanish flu continued its
deadly march. These Seattle policemen in December 1918
still wear gauze masks. *[National Archives]*

the domestics understood English and were reporting his conversations."

The chief usher at the White House, Ike Hoover, later said, "We could but surmise that something queer was happening in his mind. . . . He was never the same after this little spell of sickness."

"It is of course impossible to say what Wilson would have done had he not become sick," writes John M. Barry in his account of the epidemic. "Perhaps he would have made the concessions anyway, trading every principle away to save the League of Nations. Or perhaps he would have sailed home as he threatened to do just as he was succumbing to the disease. Then either there would have been no treaty or his walkout would have forced Clemenceau to compromise."

Wilson returned to America as a conquering hero. But his dream of a League of Nations that would help preserve peace was dashed by political opposition—and ultimately his health. As Wilson made a nationwide train trip in the fall of 1919 to muster support for the league, his health deteriorated. The campaign was canceled, and Wilson returned to the White House. There on October 2, 1919, the president suffered a stroke.

As he fought for the League of Nations treaty in the U.S. Senate, he was battling for his life. His wife, Edith Galt Wilson, and Dr. Grayson concealed the full extent of his illness from politicians, the press, and the public. He never spoke in public again, although he recovered to some degree. Ultimately, the U.S. Senate rejected the treaty and the League of Nations, dooming any chance it might have had to preserve international peace.

Fighting in the Great War may have ended in November 1918. The Spanish flu did not.

Just as they had flocked to Liberty Loan parades, crowds of people filled the streets to celebrate the end of the war. The thing health officers feared most was the result of the spontaneous celebrations. Massive crowds were converging on American streets in joy. "Health officials realized that the close contact of the celebrations would likely result in an increased number of new influenza cases," writes Julian A. Navarro. "Little could be done to prevent it. As one official in Denver put it, 'There is no use trying to lay down any rules regarding the peace celebration, as the lid is off entirely, and should be on account of the glorious ending of the world's biggest war.'"

Even as soldiers, doctors, and nurses slowly began to depart from the trenches and frontline hospitals, the battle against the pandemic continued. Doctors and researchers still struggled to find a cause and a cure. Nurses fought to keep their sick patients alive while preventing new infections. Much of their effort was in vain.

As the war ended, among the flu epidemic's ill-fated victims were young men who had refused to fight. According to World War I historian Adam Hochschild, "Influenza was the likely killer of most of the 73 British conscientious objectors who died behind bars, in alternative-service work camps, or soon after their release."

Far from the battlefields of France and Belgium, the flu pestilence continued its deadly ride around the globe. In the Fiji Islands, according to John M. Barry, 14 percent of the population died in just sixteen days between November 25 and December 10. As in many of the places where the flu had touched down, it was impossible to bury all the dead.

In North America, the flu epidemic continued through December 1918 and into the new year of 1919.

In March 1919 professional hockey's championship was called off just hours before the Montreal Canadiens and the Seattle Metropolitans were set to drop the puck in the deciding game. The teams were tied at 2–2. But players on both teams had been sidelined by the flu; five Canadiens and the manager were hospitalized. A few days later, Montreal defenseman Joe Hall died of pneumonia and complications from the flu. Today, the names of both teams are engraved on the Stanley Cup for 1919.

In 1920, the flu would return again with deadly impact, but fall short of the catastrophic toll it had taken in 1918.

"The virus burned through the available fuel," John M. Barry concludes, "then it quickly faded away."

Montreal defenseman Joe Hall died of pneumonia and complications from the Spanish flu in April 1919. [*Wikimedia*]

CHAPTER NINE

BACK TO BREVIG MISSION

*Epidemics create a kind of history from below:
they can be world-changing, but the participants are
almost inevitably ordinary folk, following their established
routines, not thinking for a second about how their
actions will be recorded for posterity. And of course,
if they do recognize that they are living through
a historical crisis, it's often too late—because,
like it or not, the primary way that ordinary people
create this distinct genre of history is by dying.*
—Steven Johnson, *The Ghost Map*

The Health Department in Rochester, New York, produced flu
warning posters in four languages. *[Rochester Public Library]*

I T WAS 1950. The horrors of the First World War were distant
memories, displaced by the calamities of World War II and
the Holocaust. In America's heartland, Johan Hultin, a twenty-
five-year-old researcher from Sweden, was studying at the
University of Iowa when he had a chance conversation over

lunch. Hultin was focused on influenza viruses and had been interested in the 1918 flu pandemic for years.

By this time, scientists had begun to unlock the secret of influenza. In the early 1930s, they proved it was caused by a virus, not the bacteria many had blamed during the pandemic. Experimental vaccines began to be developed. Through the 1940s, different strains of the virus were found, showing it could quickly mutate, changing its genetic makeup. In 1944, the U.S. Army started giving flu shots to all its soldiers. In a process still used today, the flu shots were made from viruses grown in chicken eggs, then killed so that they could not cause infection. The dead virus triggers the body's immune system response without actually making the person sick.

The lunchtime conversation with a visiting scientist from a well-known laboratory had piqued Hultin's interest. The key to unlocking the still hidden secrets of the 1918 Spanish flu, the scientist suggested, might lie with bodies buried in an Arctic region where the permanently frozen ground might keep the viruses intact. Intrigued, Hultin later hit on the idea of going to Alaska to find bodies of flu victims that might be buried in the permafrost.

Lacking both funding and serious scientific equipment, Hultin became obsessed with his quest. When he learned of the place called Brevig Mission, he traveled there in 1951 and discovered the graves of the village's victims, marked by a pair of crosses. Following a hunch, Hultin spoke with some of the village elders about his search for an answer to the Purple Death, and he was given permission to dig.

"This was a great adventure for a little boy from Sweden," he told the *San Francisco Chronicle* in a 2001 interview. "I had never spoken to Eskimos before. I thought I was going to find the virus alive, I really did."

The man who traveled to Alaska in search of the Spanish flu virus, Johan Hultin was later called the "Indiana Jones of the scientific set." [Kim Komenich, San Francisco Chronicle]

After the catastrophe hit Brevig Mission, few survivors were left to bury the dead. Fewer still wanted to go near the bodies. Eventually, Alaskan territorial officials hired gold miners from Nome to bury the remains of flu victims in 1919. Using steam machinery, they melted a hole twelve feet wide, twenty-five feet long, and about six feet deep in the frozen ground.

Now in 1951, the bodies remained encased in the frozen soil. Working alone at first with only a pickax and shovel,

Hultin built a fire to thaw the rock-hard ground, shoveled off the melted soil, then repeated the process. "It took two days to reach the first body," he later recalled.

Two scientists from the University of Iowa and a paleontologist from the university in Fairbanks joined Hultin. Wearing only surgical masks and gloves, they had little protection against the virus if it should somehow still be "live." Using the picks for two more days, the men reached four more bodies.

"In 1951, I was a graduate student," Hultin later explained to journalist Gina Kolata. "I just didn't have enough knowledge of how things spread. . . . We took precautions that were standard at the time, but we were not afraid of getting infected."

Working with the remains of the flu victims, Hultin used rib cutters—instruments that look like pruning shears—to remove the chest plates and expose the lungs of the frozen corpses. Then he snipped some of the tissue from the lungs.

"We probably had a two-inch cube from each lung. The reason we didn't do more was that we had a limited number of specimen containers." The effort was decidedly low-tech and improvised. Using sterilized screw-cap jars, Hultin managed to get the lung tissue samples back to a lab in Iowa City. Without proper refrigeration equipment, he had preserved the tissue samples with dry ice removed from fire extinguishers. Back in the Iowa laboratory, however, using what would now be considered primitive techniques, Hultin failed to produce any live virus.

More than forty years later, in March 1997, fate struck again. Having retired as a pathologist, Johan Hultin happened to come across an article in *Science* magazine about other scientists seeking the answer to the Spanish flu mystery. One of these researchers, Dr. Jeffery Taubenberger, had discovered Spanish flu virus in tissue samples from 1918—a tiny bit of lung tissue that had been kept in storage by the U.S. Army. During the 1918 pandemic, doctors in the army camps had performed autopsies and collected tiny samples of lung tissue. A doctor in Fort Riley in Kansas—site of the initial outbreak in March 1918—had dutifully preserved the lung tissue in paraffin wax and sent it to Washington, D.C., where it lay in storage for nearly eighty years. "It was like *Raiders of the Lost Ark*," Taubenberger later said. "We found the Ark of the Covenant."

Reviving his quest, Hultin contacted Taubenberger and volunteered to go back to Alaska. Using his own savings, the seventy-two-year-old Hultin struck out for Brevig Mission once more in August 1997. The tissue samples from 1951 were by now useless. He would need to find new samples. On this solitary expedition, the veteran pathologist carried a pair of garden clippers borrowed, without permission, from his wife.

At about the same time, another research team was attempting to find the remains of the virus in the bodies of miners buried on a Norwegian island. That attempt failed when they discovered the ground in which the bodies were buried had thawed and refrozen repeatedly over the years.

As he had done in 1951, Johan Hultin appealed to the villagers for permission to open the graves. Again, Hultin explained his mission to the people, including the niece of a 1918 victim. "I said that a terrible thing had happened in November 1918 and I am here to ask permission to go back to the grave for a second time," Hultin later recalled. "Science has now moved to the point where it is possible to analyze a dead virus and through that make a vaccine so that when it comes again, all of you can be immunized against it. There shouldn't be any more mass deaths."

With the agreement of local leaders and help from four young men of the village, Hultin opened the mass grave once more and found the body of a large woman who had died in the Spanish flu epidemic.

Hultin named the woman Lucy, taking his inspiration from the discovery of an ancient skeleton found in Ethiopia in 1974 that shed light on human evolution. The corpse's thick layers of fat kept the woman's lungs well preserved in the permafrost.

Using his wife's pruning shears, Hultin opened Lucy's mummified rib cage. He found two frozen lungs—the tissue he needed—and both were still full of blood. He removed the lungs, sliced them with an autopsy knife, and placed them in preserving fluid provided by Dr. Taubenberger.

Then he and the village helpers replaced the graveyard sod. Noticing that the grave markers from 1951 were gone, Hultin went to a nearby woodshop and built two new crosses. Carefully documenting the names of the seventy-two Brevig flu victims, Hultin later paid for brass plaques honoring the people whose deaths might now help unlock the secret of the Spanish flu. The plaques were attached to the crosses he had made.

With the samples Hultin had collected and sent on, a breakthrough moment was at hand. But it was not going to be an overnight solution. Using far more sophisticated techniques than had been available in 1951, including more advanced understanding of genetics and the ability to "map" genes, the secret of the Spanish flu virus was about to be unlocked.

Years of painstaking work led to a development that was a little like something out of *Jurassic Park*. Jeffery Taubenberger, medical technician Ann Reid, and their colleagues finally reconstructed the 1918 Spanish flu virus in 2005. Working with Hultin's samples, the 1918 lung samples from Camp Funston preserved in paraffin, and another sample of the virus from the Royal London Hospital, Taubenberger and his colleagues actually re-created the virus in a secure lab at the Centers for Disease Control and Prevention. These researchers used it to infect mice and human lung cells that had been grown in lab dishes. "For the first time in history," writes science journalist Gina Kolata, "a long-extinct virus had been resurrected."

One of the mysteries of the Spanish flu was solved: it was an avian strain of influenza, a virus carried by birds, which had jumped directly to humans.

"When a pathogen [a microorganism that can cause disease] leaps from some nonhuman animal into a person . . . sometimes causing illness or death, the result is a zoonosis," science writer David Quammen explains. "It's a mildly technical term . . . but it helps clarify the biological complexities behind the ominous headlines about swine flu, bird flu, SARS, emerging diseases in general, and the threat of a global pandemic. It helps us comprehend why medical science and public health campaigns have been able to conquer some horrific diseases, such as smallpox and polio, but unable to conquer other horrific diseases, such as dengue and yellow fever. . . . Ebola is a zoonosis. So is bubonic plague. So was the so-called Spanish influenza of 1918–1919."

Besides isolating, identifying, and re-creating the Spanish flu virus, there were still large questions to be answered: Why was the virus so deadly? Why did it strike the young and healthy? And where did it really come from?

There are several possible explanations for the high mortality rate of the 1918 influenza pandemic. One is that a mutation of this particular virus had made the Spanish flu particularly aggressive. Viruses are in a constant state of mutation, as they exist only to find hosts in which they can reproduce. These alterations in the influenza virus mean a new flu vaccine is required each year to respond to the changes. As Jeffery Taubenberger writes, "It is unclear what gave the 1918 virus this unusual ability to generate repeated waves of illness. Perhaps the surface proteins of the virus drifted more rapidly than other influenza virus strains, or perhaps the virus had an unusually effective mechanism for evading the human immune system."

The most obvious factor is that wartime circumstances alone contributed to the extraordinarily high death toll. Malnutrition, overcrowding in army and refugee camps, hospitals, and poor hygiene all combined to create large groups highly susceptible to the flu and far less able to fight it off.

That doesn't explain why the Spanish flu was so strangely fatal to younger people. "Influenza and pneumonia death rates for 15-to-34-year-olds," Taubenberger explains, "were more than twenty times higher in 1918 than in previous years."

It may have to do with the power of the immune system. Younger, healthier people tend to have stronger immune systems. The immune system is the body's response to any sort of danger. It is now thought that the powerful immune reactions of young adults were simply too strong. Part of their immune response was to send body fluids, including blood, to the lungs to attack or dislodge the invading virus. As the immune systems of young people aggressively responded to the virus, large amounts of bloody fluid flooded the lungs. Younger people, including many soldiers, were drowning in their own bodily fluids—the cause of the cyanosis that turned victims blue—the direct cause of the deaths of so many flu victims. The weaker immune systems of children and middle-aged adults resulted in fewer deaths among those groups.

This idea was tested in monkeys infected with the virus in 2007. The virus quickly spread and set off a powerful immune system response, moving faster than a normal flu virus and filling their lungs with blood and other fluids. The same thing may have happened to healthy humans in 1918. "Essentially people are drowned by themselves," said one of the researchers in the monkey experiment.

There is another theory that explains the high mortality rates in 1918 and 1919. Perhaps the Spanish flu virus was not brand-new in 1918 but had existed before in a slightly weaker form. Some people may have already been affected by a strain of this flu virus and had developed the necessary antibodies—a protein produced by the immune system to fight viruses—to fend off the Spanish flu.

The question of the Spanish flu's geographical origin still remains a mystery. If the Spanish flu existed before 1918, it could have originated in several places before exploding in Haskell County, Kansas, in March 1918. There had been earlier outbreaks of a similar flu in China and France. But lacking tissue samples from anyone in those areas, this remains an unsolved question. One theory is that the virus responsible for the Spanish flu was carried by wild aquatic birds. After passing through domesticated animals, such as ducks, it eventually made the leap to humans—perhaps through an open wound or small cut on someone handling infected bird meat or through consuming infected poultry.

AS THE SPANISH FLU epidemic wound down, the scientists who had struggled to understand it were brought up short. Dr. Victor Vaughan was one of the leading medical authorities of the time. He had seen the carnage of the pandemic in its early days at Camp Devens in the autumn of 1918. After the Spanish flu pandemic began to recede, he said, "Never again allow me to say that medical science is on the verge of conquering disease. . . . Doctors know no more about this flu than 14th century Florentine doctors had known about the Black Death."

While some mysteries of the Spanish flu are still being explored, the consequences of the pandemic were profound in America and around the world.

The New Testament book of Revelation describes the Four Horsemen of the Apocalypse, whose arrival signals widespread disaster and destruction for humanity. Following World War I, two of these biblical Four Horsemen—War and Disease—had completed a hard ride over the world's landscape. The life expectancy in America, which had been rising for decades, suddenly fell in 1918 from fifty-one years to thirty-nine years, dropping by an astonishing twelve years. The year 1918 also showed a very rare decline in the American population. Hundreds of thousands of children had been orphaned and whole families wiped out. Besides the unthinkable human toll, businesses had been destroyed and fortunes lost in the death and destruction.

After the twin horrors of world war and the Spanish flu, many Americans longed for a return to normalcy—a word used by President Warren G. Harding in his successful 1920 campaign for the presidency. It may be one of the reasons that very few people wrote or talked about the Spanish flu and that it largely disappeared from public memory—becoming a piece of hidden history.

In many ways, America turned inward again. The horrors of the war and fears of rising Bolshevism in Eastern Europe made many Americans wary of immigrants and foreign entanglements. The desire to return to the isolationism of the past was expressed in stark terms when the U.S. Senate overwhelmingly rejected American membership in the League of

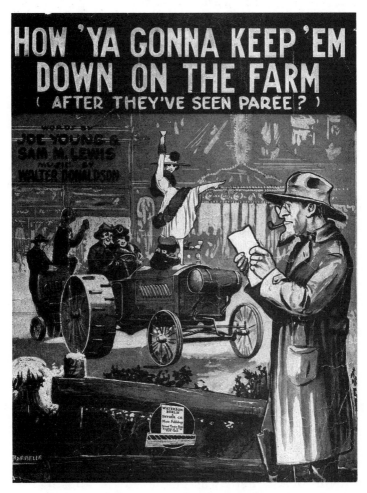

Cover of sheet music for the popular song
"How 'Ya Gonna Keep 'Em Down on the Farm."
[Wikimedia]

Nations. Without American participation, Woodrow Wilson's idealistic dream of a world body that would promote and protect international peace was doomed to ineffectiveness.

America soon passed stricter immigration laws targeting Italians, Jews, and other people from Eastern Europe. The Ku Klux Klan, a racist terrorist group born out of the defeated Confederacy, was revived in the 1920s. Alongside its traditional hatred of African Americans, the invigorated Klan had a new emphasis on keeping foreigners, especially Catholics and Jews, out of America.

Laws were also passed to battle what was seen as a growing threat of socialism after the Russian Revolution created the communist Soviet state. During the war, the Justice Department had created the Alien Enemy Bureau to keep track of the half million Germans on American soil. After the war, America underwent what was called the Red Scare of 1919–1920, when federal authorities in the Justice Department's General Intelligence Division arrested thousands in an effort to round up suspected socialists, anarchists, and radicals. Although the department was criticized for abusing Americans' civil rights during this period, most Americans were reassured. The intelligence division was later folded into the Justice Department's Bureau of Investigation, now known as the FBI.

Even though many wanted to forget the horrors of the Spanish flu—in what medical journalist Gina Kolata later called "collective amnesia"—America had been changed. Part of the response was to enter a new era, what would be called the Jazz Age and Roaring Twenties. The booming stock market on Wall Street was the centerpiece of a new American economy that seemed to know no limits. The country was firing on all cylinders as the Automobile Age began and America sped into the twentieth century.

While the nation wanted normalcy, it also wanted to forget its recent troubles. As people left farms for factories and began moving to growing cities, a popular song of the time asked, "How 'ya gonna keep 'em down on the farm (after they've seen Paree)?"

In art and fashion, the world was becoming thoroughly modern. Radio stations blared the new music called jazz. "Moving picture" theaters, some of which had been shuttered during the pandemic, sprouted across the country as Hollywood became America's entertainment center.

American women, in particular, tossed aside many traditions and conventions. New hairstyles, "flapper" dresses, and "shocking" dances like the Charleston appeared. As wartime had pushed more women into the workforce, many were beginning to look toward careers and professional lives. The large number of nurses enlisted in the flu effort had changed what had once been a volunteer job into a more established profession. And in 1920, American women finally got the right to vote with ratification of the Nineteenth Amendment to the Constitution.

Many of the women who marched and demonstrated for the vote were also pressing for Prohibition—outlawing alcohol. A belief that the nation had become too criminal and violent because of widespread drunkenness had led to ratification of the Eighteenth Amendment to the Constitution in 1919.

American medicine was also undergoing a transformation. The Spanish flu pandemic had underscored the importance of serious scientific research. Once far behind the standards of European medical and scientific research, American universities and government agencies gradually modernized and upgraded America's scientific facilities. "Around the world, authorities made plans for international cooperation on health," writes John M. Barry, "and the experience led to restructuring public health efforts throughout the United States." Working without the United States, the League of Nations created its Health Section in 1922, with a focus on coordinating international quarantines to limit the spread of contagion in the war's aftermath. (It was the forerunner of the current United Nations' World Health Organization, or WHO.) The public gradually forgot the specter of the Spanish flu, but research into the flu and other diseases continued. It took Congress ten years to finally pass legislation in 1930 that created the National Institute of Health, establishing a new era of federal support for medical and scientific research.

*We can only conclude that since it happened once,
analogous conditions could lead to an
equally devastating pandemic.*
—Jeffery K. Taubenberger and David M. Morens, 2006

T HE WAR THAT climaxed in November 1918 and the Spanish flu went hand in hand. There is little doubt that wartime conditions were responsible for allowing the Spanish flu to move so far and so fast. There is also little question that the Spanish flu had a considerable impact on the course of the war. But even without a global war going on today, the frightening history of the Spanish flu leaves a last but most pressing question. And it certainly must keep some researchers up at night.

Could it come back?

Since 1918, enormous strides in medicine have limited or eliminated many of the most threatening diseases, whether from viruses or other sources. But recently around the planet, several major flu and other viral outbreaks have prompted

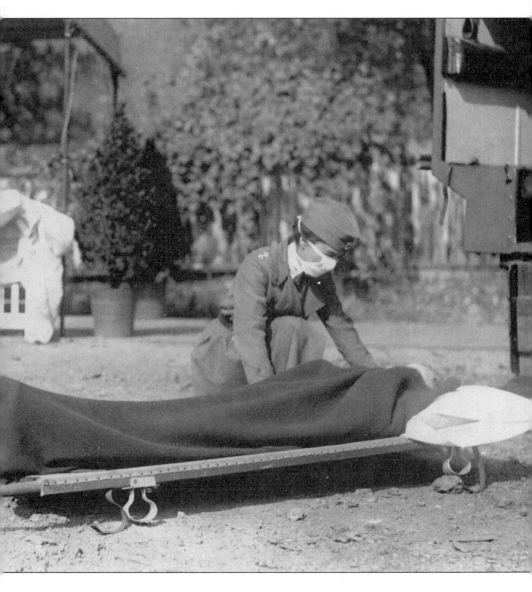

A Red Cross nurse demonstrates treatment practices in 1918.

[Library of Congress]

such worries. The globalization of trade has large container ships plying the oceans; high-speed transportation can move disease carriers swiftly around the world on jets and trains; booming population growth is taking place in some developing nations; and natural disasters are all too frequent. All of these factors change the risk equation for a pandemic. On top of all these variables, climate change may be the most severe.

In 1997, an outbreak of avian, or bird, flu originating in Hong Kong led to the destruction of 1.5 million farm birds, possibly averting another much greater human pandemic. From 2002 to 2004, a new viral disease called SARS (Severe Acute Respiratory Syndrome) appeared and began to spread rapidly from south China to several major cities around the world. Traced to wild civet cats, the virus created a near panic. But extraordinary efforts to curb the epidemic succeeded, as travelers from Asia were carefully screened at airports and other checkpoints.

The rise of international terrorism and the use of banned chemical weapons in conflicts such as Syria's civil war also raises the specter of a deliberately linked outbreak of war and disease. Terrorists in Japan once used a nerve agent in the Tokyo subways. Anthrax, a serious and potentially deadly illness caused by bacteria and most commonly found in farm animals, has also been used as a chemical weapon as far back as World War I. In the wake of the 9/11 terror attacks in the

United States, envelopes containing spores of anthrax were mailed to television stations and members of Congress, killing five people. After a long manhunt, the man ultimately suspected of mailing the deadly packages was identified as a worker in an army biochemical lab. He committed suicide, and the FBI confirmed that he was the culprit after his death. The U.S. Postal Service installed biohazard detection systems at its major distribution centers after these events to scan for anthrax in the mail.

An outbreak of cholera in Haiti, introduced to the impoverished island nation in 2010 by United Nations peacekeepers, worsened in 2016 after Hurricane Matthew. Flooding rivers and streams quickly spread the disease. The storm largely destroyed much of the already meager water and sanitation infrastructure in Haiti's southwest, leaving it ripe for a new cholera outbreak. A vaccination campaign in the aftermath of the storm will help, but it will not address the much-needed improvements in sanitation and water treatment facilities.

In China, avian flu began spreading once more among wild and domesticated bird flocks in 2003. In early 2017, Chinese authorities were again battling a surge in bird flu infections, shutting down live poultry markets across the country after the disease killed dozens of people. The strain, identified as H7N9, is an avian influenza virus that can infect people who come in close contact with infected live or newly killed birds.

That outbreak came on the heels of a round of avian flu that struck Canada and the United States in 2014 through 2016. When the Moline family, turkey farmers in Iowa, went to bed one night in May 2015, their fifty-six thousand turkeys were healthy; the next morning, almost a hundred were dead, and hundreds more were gasping for breath. Thousands of birds died in days.

"I'd never seen anything like it before," Brad Moline told science and food writer Maryn McKenna. "My father, who is 70 years old, he'd never seen anything like it before, and some older relatives that have been around this area for a long time, they'd never seen anything like it. It rolled through the farm like a runaway train." About one hundred miles away, McKenna writes, Rembrandt Foods, an egg-producer, had to destroy more than eight million birds.

The global spread of an outbreak of a different sort made international headlines as Brazil prepared to welcome the world to the Olympic Games in the summer of 2016. The Zika virus, spread by a type of mosquito, affected pregnant women most dangerously and was responsible for serious birth defects. As some fearful athletes chose not to participate in the games, the Zika virus began to move rapidly across the Americas, especially in tropical areas, including the Caribbean. Governments warned women to avoid or postpone pregnancy.

Since then, Zika has waned almost everywhere in the

Western Hemisphere, according to *Washington Post* reporters Marina Lopes and Nick Miroff. "Epidemiologists say the pattern fits the typical trajectory of a virus that spreads explosively at first but fizzles out as it runs out of new hosts to infect," they write. Even so, Zika left thousands of children suffering from severe and devastating birth defects.

What also alarms many scientists is the growing concern that Zika is one of many insect-borne diseases that will worsen as a result of climate change. Journalist Maryn McKenna writes in "Why the Menace of Mosquitoes Will Only Get Worse":

> *The unpredictable weather patterns stimulated by climate change affect infectious diseases, as well as chronic ones. Warmer weather encourages food-borne organisms like salmonella to multiply more rapidly, and warmer seas foster the growth of bacteria like Vibrio that make oysters unsafe to eat. Spikes in heat and humidity have less visible effects, too, changing the numbers and distribution of the insect intermediaries that carry diseases to people.*

DESPITE THE ADVANCES made in disease control and prevention, and vaccines that protect against many infections, the spread of diseases like Zika is what scientists fear most. Moving from the insect and animal world to the human population, such contagions represent major health threats. In 2015, malaria killed more than four hundred thousand people around the world. Most of them are children under the age of five, mainly in sub-Saharan Africa.

In their article describing the resurrection of the Spanish flu virus, Jeffery Taubenberger and David M. Morens write, "We can only conclude that since it happened once, analogous conditions could lead to an equally devastating pandemic. . . . Understanding influenza pandemics in general requires understanding the 1918 pandemic in all its historical, epidemiologic, and biologic aspects."

History and science are fairly clear on this point: another pandemic is a distinct possibility. Viruses are a treacherous enemy. An international scientific community that is focused on prevention, containment, and new treatments is constantly at work on solutions.

Improved and newly developed vaccines, including those that can be inhaled, are being produced. A new vaccine against a diarrheal disease that kills some six hundred children a day worked well in a large trial in Africa, according to the *New York Times*. "The new vaccine against rotavirus, the most common cause of death from diarrhea in children under age 5, . . . is expected to be as cheap as or cheaper than current alternatives. More important, it can last for months without refrigeration, which makes it far easier to use in remote villages with no electricity."

New generations of antiviral drugs have also proven to be effective. But viruses adapt and mutate, becoming resistant to some of these drugs. It is a constant battle to stay ahead of them.

The best steps that most of us can take are fairly simple, according to John M. Barry, including the simplest of all: washing our hands. "The virus can remain on a hard surface—a doorknob, say—for hours. It can be transmitted if someone opens a door, then rubs his or her eyes or covers a yawn."

The Centers for Disease Control and Prevention offers two other pieces of very simple advice: cover your coughs and stay home from school or work when you are seriously ill. The use of masks is recommended for people who are already sick to protect other people from being infected, but they are not advised for most people as a preventive measure. (A complete CDC list of preventive measures follows in Appendix 2.)

It is also important to continue to remain educated and make every effort to be well informed. In assessing the way governments and the press may have worsened the 1918 pandemic by concealing the truth about the flu, John M. Barry concludes that the public was misled about the risks, often by diminishing the flu's threat in the hopes of preventing panic, or optimistically reporting the pandemic's end. Some of the most sensational press reports spread fear: "So a terror seeped into the society that prevented one woman from caring for her sister, that prevented volunteers from bringing food to families too ill to feed themselves and who starved to death because of it, that prevented trained nurses from responding to the most urgent calls for their services. The fear, not the disease, threatened to break the society apart."

The twin scourges of war and disease have always existed side by side. Governments, religious groups, political parties, and others have often used misleading or outright false information to influence political opinion and shape policy. Propaganda has often created hatred and spread anxiety.

When the Great War broke out, propaganda made people fear other nations by calling them "barbaric." In 1918, people were panicked by a disease they did not understand. Many had been told that an enemy was spreading the flu. In some respects, the linked stories of the Spanish flu and World War I are about ignorance and fear—what Spanish flu survivor President Franklin D. Roosevelt later described in another crisis as the "nameless, unreasoning, unjustified terror which paralyzes needed efforts to convert retreat into advance."

As this book was being written, the issues of "fake news" and "alternative facts" filled the media and worldwide conversation. Much of that discussion revolved around politics. The heated debates involved refugees and immigrants, who were often being unfairly blamed for spreading crime, disease, and terror. Some of the controversy over fake news also concerned questions about lifesaving vaccines, dangers from new diseases, and the scientifically established threat of human-induced global climate change.

Climate change and the issue of global warming became a political issue and a subject of debate in America's presidential race in 2016. But to the vast majority of scientists, the facts behind these issues are not a question of serious debate. "Climate change is turning abnormal weather into a common occurrence," Maryn McKenna wrote in early 2017. "Anything that improves conditions for mosquitoes tips the scales for the diseases they carry as well: the West Nile virus that flattened Dallas, the dengue that returned to Florida in 2009 after 63 years and the newest arrival, Zika, which gained a toehold in the United States last year and is expected to surge this summer."

The change in climate trends became even more alarming when the budget announced by the new administration in 2017 included deep cuts to the National Institutes of Health, including a network of researchers who are on the lookout for viral threats. They are part of the nation's "early-warning system" for an attack not by nuclear missiles but by dangerous diseases that will spread as the planet warms. Tropical diseases "know no borders," Dr. Chris Beyrer, professor of public health at Johns Hopkins University, warned in the *New York Times.* "America is not hived off from the rest of the planet, and it's incredibly important to our biosecurity to have surveillance capability—which means partners in other countries."

In other words, ignorance, propaganda, and the deliberate resistance to scientific facts are extremely dangerous attitudes. Many current controversial views—on politics, religion, or immigrants—have been around for a long time. Over the centuries, different ethnic and religious groups in America and other countries have often been unfairly regarded with fear and suspicion. In America's past, Germans, Irish, Italians, Poles, Chinese, and Japanese—as well as religious groups including Catholics, Jews, and more recently Muslims—have all been singled out as threats. We should understand that fact is an important part of history if we hope to do a better job of overcoming prejudice.

The same idea holds for science. While researchers warn about the potential return of another flu pandemic, some established medical facts about vaccines are being challenged. That makes it more important than ever to be cautious or even skeptical about our sources of information. Facts matter. The truth matters. We must safeguard medical facts based on soundly gathered evidence and not allow unsubstantiated opinions to blur scientific knowledge.

One lesson of the Spanish flu is that information, education, and cooperation are the best antidote to fend off ignorance and propaganda. In that sense, the story of the Spanish flu is about truth. It is about how important it is to guard against that unreasoning terror that has no basis in fact or science. It is about the cost of ignorance. Understanding established facts and relying on knowledge to counteract fake news and outright propaganda is one of the most important lessons to be learned from the story of the Spanish flu.

APPENDIX 1

MIASMAS, MICROBES, AND MOSQUITOES

A Brief History and Time Line of Disease and Medicine

The winners of past wars were not always the armies
with the best generals and weapons, but were often
merely those bearing the nastiest germs
to transmit to their enemies.
—Jared Diamond, *Guns, Germs, and Steel*

For almost two centuries, the knowledge that the world
teemed with small organisms was regarded as an
interesting but rather irrelevant fact.
—Kathryn Senior, 2017

WAR AND DISEASE. From the first syllable of recorded time, these twin plagues have ridden side by side through history and literature. Homer's epic *Iliad* opens as a deadly illness—Apollo's arrows—cuts down the Greek army camped on the shores of Troy. In the book of Exodus, the ten plagues end when the angel of death strikes Egypt's firstborn in a single

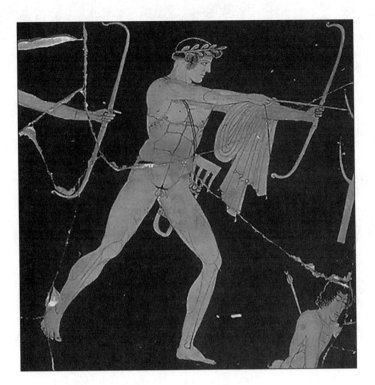

The god Apollo, depicted here on an ancient Greek vase, shoots plague arrows at the Greeks in the opening scene of Homer's *Iliad*. *[Louvre Museum]*

horrific night. And after a battle in the first book of Samuel, deadly tumors attack the Philistines who capture the Ark of the Covenant—ancient Israel's most sacred possession.

But lethal outbreaks of sickness, often linked to conflict, have played a role that goes far beyond biblical stories and ancient poetry. War and disease are both powerful forces in shaping events. While historians and schoolbooks tend to

The Death of the Pharaoh's Firstborn (1872)
by Lawrence Alma-Tademah. The original painting
is in Amsterdam's Rijksmuseum. *[Wikimedia]*

focus on the warfare and what Shakespeare called "the evil that men do," killer epidemics have often played a much larger part in shaping many of civilization's significant moments.

The Ancient World

ONE OF THE MOST famous battles in Western history was fought at Thermopylae in 480 BCE. During a war between the Greeks and Persia, a force of three hundred legendary

Spartan warriors heroically held off an enormous Persian army. Depicted in the popular 2006 film *300*, based on a graphic novel series, the struggle is presented as a gory, R-rated tableau of a small group of muscled men, armed with javelins, fending off countless hordes of Persian fighters, some mounted on armored elephants, and raining what seems like millions of arrows down on the hopelessly outnumbered Spartans.

But according to the Greek historian Herodotus, the Persians may have been stopped in their tracks by something less heroic. Their invading army suffered from an epidemic of dysentery—an intestinal disease usually spread by contaminated drinking water. This debilitating and often deadly affliction brings on severe stomach cramps and bloody diarrhea. Those symptoms sound far less exciting than the saga of a suicidal stand of a group of doomed warriors wielding swords, spears, and shields. But dysentery may have helped tip the scales in a war considered a turning point in Western history.

Half a century later, the Greek historian Thucydides described an epidemic that devastated Athens during a long war fought between the cities of Athens and Sparta. In his *History of the Peloponnesian War*, Thucydides detailed what is considered the first recorded pandemic:

> *People in good health were all of a sudden attacked by violent heats in the head, and redness and inflammation in the eyes,*

the inward parts, such as the throat or tongue, becoming
bloody and emitting an unnatural and fetid breath.

LASTING FIVE YEARS, this highly contagious epidemic broke out in early May 430 BCE, with another wave coming in the summer of 428 BCE and a third in the winter of 427–426 BCE. Over that time, this plague may have killed a quarter of the population in overcrowded Athens, the most deadly outbreak of disease recorded to that time.

Just as Americans wondered in 1918 if the Germans had poisoned their water, the people of Athens suspected the Spartans of polluting their wells. What else would explain the sudden onslaught of a mysterious disease that killed Pericles, the city's famed leader? Thucydides himself fell sick but survived to recount scenes of temples filled with corpses, and bodies lying on top of one another. Describing a collapse of civil society in Athens, Thucydides wrote, "Men, not knowing what was to become of them, became utterly careless of everything, whether sacred or profane." People soon simply began tossing the bodies of family and friends on top of random burning piles of remains being cremated.

Thucydides also depicted scenes of people plunging into rain barrels to cool their fevers and relieve unquenchable thirst. The medicines of the day were useless. So were Athenian physicians who fell after coming into contact with the sick:

They died themselves the most thickly, as they visited the sick most often; nor did any human art succeed any better. Supplications in the temples, divinations, and so forth were found equally futile, till the overwhelming nature of the disaster at last put a stop to them altogether.

LIKE OTHER GREEKS of his time, Thucydides began to ask questions. He wanted to know where and how the pandemic began. According to Thucydides, the disease had traveled from Ethiopia, passed through Egypt and Libya, and entered the Greek world through seaports used by Athenians. Thinking scientifically, he tried to remove the notions of supernatural influences as the causes of deadly disease outbreaks. The gods of Mount Olympus—Zeus and his thunderbolts, Apollo's deadly arrows—could not be punishing humanity.

Thucydides was following the example of Hippocrates, a man who is regarded as the father of Western medicine. A somewhat fabled figure, Hippocrates was reportedly born on the isle of Kos and lived between 460 BCE and 375 BCE— around the time of the Peloponnesian War. Although much of his life story exists only in legend, Hippocrates is mentioned in the famous dialogs of the philosophers Plato and Aristotle. As a physician, he believed in focusing on the patient rather than the disease. He is also famed for inspiring the phrase "First, do no harm," reflecting the idea that a physician's first responsibility was not to do anything to injure a patient. However, these oft-repeated words were never part of the Hippocratic Oath, once required of medical students becoming doctors but no longer widely recited by physicians.

Hippocratic methods rejected ancient ideas about health and disease. People did not become ill merely because they had offended the gods or failed to make the correct offerings of sacrificial animals or votive gifts—small statuettes, spearheads, or other everyday items of value. "Prayer indeed is good," Hippocrates wrote, "but while calling on the gods a man should himself lend a hand."

Hippocrates and others like Thucydides sought natural causes for disease, but they were working in the dark, with no practical sense of the workings of the human body. At that time Greeks considered performing autopsies of the dead taboo, an attitude that would later change with the establishment of a school of Greek medicine in the third century BCE. They also had no concept about microscopic organisms that caused illness.

Instead, Hippocrates and his followers relied upon observation to form their ideas of health and sickness. Among the most influential of these concepts was the mistaken notion that the human body was composed of four "humors" or fluids: blood, phlegm, black bile, and yellow bile, or choler. Good health, according to Hippocrates and physicians from the classical era right into the late nineteenth century, depended on keeping these humors in balance; an imbalance in the humors caused disease.

The humors could be thrown out of balance by many things, including bad diet, drinking too much, or even a dog bite. Regulating the diet and purging—using drugs or other means to stimulate the bowels or to induce vomiting—were among the regimens used to assist healing. Another way of dealing with an imbalance of the humors was removing a quantity of blood—a process called bloodletting, also widely used until the late nineteenth century.

Thucydides never found the cause of the Athens plague, a disease whose identity remains a mystery to this day. Still, the epidemic altered the outcome of the Peloponnesian War and history. Ravaged by sickness, death, and a war the Athenians could no longer fight, the golden age of Athens came to a crashing end. Believing that the gods favored Sparta in the conflict, Athenians doubted their religious beliefs. People began to hole up in their homes, fearful of visiting neighbors, and unwilling to help the sick. "Whatever this pestilence may have been," writes medical historian Lois N. Magner, "it provides a striking example of the recurrent theme of social disintegration linked to war and epidemic diseases."

At another of classical history's great turning points, disease may have cut down one of the ancient world's great conquerors. Alexander the Great of Macedonia had fought wars

The practice of bloodletting is depicted on an ancient Greek vase from circa 480-470 BCE. [Wikimedia]

and marched his armies across continents, establishing an empire that spanned from Greece as far into Asia as India and across the Mediterranean into Egypt. He was a military genius who conquered many lands. But he was not brought down in mortal combat on the field of battle. When Alexander died in 323 BCE in Mesopotamia—modern-day Iraq—many believed that he had been poisoned.

It is far more likely that an infectious disease such as

typhus or malaria did in the warrior king, who was described as suffering from a high fever. Epidemics had already decimated the army that Alexander had taken to India in his quest for a world empire. Great armies like Alexander's, or the later Roman legions that conquered Europe and the Mediterranean world, suffered from diseases and spread deadly contagion everywhere they marched.

Ancient Rome's far-reaching and powerful realm would learn this too well. The beating heart of a far-flung empire connected by its sophisticated system of carefully constructed roads, Rome would suffer a series of plagues. As the city became a great capital, crowded with people and exotic animals from every corner of an expansive empire, a pandemic swept through the Roman Empire during the years 164–180 CE. Possibly a simultaneous attack of smallpox and measles, this was the first of several deadly waves of disease that ravaged Rome and its territories.

By far, the most lethal of these was a pandemic that began in 541 CE during the reign of Byzantine Emperor Justinian in Constantinople (modern-day Istanbul). At its peak, the Justinian plague killed five thousand people a day. It spread from the eastern half of the Roman Empire in modern-day Turkey across Europe, as far as Spain and Ireland. The illness was characterized by swollen buboes—walnut- or egg-sized blisters or sores now recognized as swollen lymph nodes—that appeared in the groins, armpits, and necks of the victims.

Milestones in Medical History

2400 BCE Egyptian mummies from the Old Kingdom era show signs of tuberculosis.

c. 1500 BCE Egypt is struck by several major disasters, including human and animal plagues, according to the biblical book of Exodus.

14th Century BCE A plague lasting twenty years devastates the Hittites (of modern-day Turkey). It may be smallpox, possibly carried by Egyptian prisoners of war.

c. 1157–1143 BCE Egyptian pharaoh Ramses V dies of smallpox, based on evidence from his mummified remains.

452 BCE Rome is devastated by a highly contagious epidemic that kills half the population.

c. 430–427 BCE The still-mysterious plague of Athens breaks out, affecting the outcome of the Peloponnesian War between Athens and Sparta.

48 CE Smallpox first appears in China.

541 The plague of Justinian strikes the Byzantine city of Constantinople, where five thousand people die every day. The epidemic coincides with the final decline of the Roman Empire.

The enormous death toll in Justinian's plague was complicated by religion. Christianity had been established as the official religion in the Roman world and, under Christian law, cremation of the dead was forbidden. Mass burial pits had to be dug, and legions of corpse-bearers were employed to carry away the bodies. This meant that the living were coming into prolonged contact with the infected dead, increasing the chances of spreading more disease. One witness, John of

In this 1500 German engraving, a plague victim points to the swollen "buboes" in his armpits. These were the most visible signs of the bubonic plague. [Library of Congress]

Ephesus, described gravediggers piling bodies oozing pus and pressing them down "as a man might heap up hay in a stack."

The plague of Justinian is thought to be the first known appearance of the disease that later came to be known simply as the plague or the Black Death. History's most notorious pandemic, the Black Death struck from 1346 to 1352 and transformed medieval Europe, Asia, and Africa. Originating in Asia, the Black Death followed trade routes—such as the fabled Silk Road—reaching Italy in 1347 aboard a merchant ship whose entire crew had been infected by the time it reached port. Around this time, there are also accounts of disease-ridden corpses being catapulted into besieged cities—a very early example of biological warfare.

The plague has three different variations: bubonic plague, the most common, in which the signs were sudden fevers and chills, headache and muscle aches, and most notably, the hard, painful swollen lymph nodes, or buboes, in the groin, neck, and armpits; septicemic plague, with bleeding from the mouth, nose, and rectum, and the blackening—caused by gangrene—of fingers, toes, and nose; and pneumonic plague, distinguished by a bloody cough, and usually fatal within two days. The plague also caused mental confusion, depression, hallucinations, and coma. Spread directly from person to person by saliva droplets in coughs and sneezes, it was highly deadly.

Plague is a disease of crowds, like most contagions. That's why some of Europe's most densely populated cities—including London, Paris, and Florence—were so ripe for epidemic. As the disease struck the surrounding areas, food production fell. With markets empty of bread and meat, malnutrition grew, making city dwellers even more susceptible to the plague.

The world had been shaken to its foundations, and the plague was visible everywhere. "Every morning, the streets were filled with bodies beyond number," writes medical historian Lois N. Magner. "Customary funeral rites were abandoned; corpses were dumped into trenches and covered with a little dirt. Famine followed plague, because peasants were too demoralized by fear to care for their crops or their animals."

The millions of plague victims included a woman named Laura, whose death moved the Italian Renaissance poet Petrarch to write his famous sonnets in her memory.

> She ruled in beauty o'er this heart of mine,
> A noble lady in a humble home,
> And now her time for
> heavenly bliss has come,
> 'Tis I am mortal proved, and she divine.

ANOTHER ITALIAN WRITER, Giovanni Boccaccio, was inspired to write his *Decameron*, a collection of stories told by ten people who take shelter in a villa outside Florence as plague sweeps the city. Each of these refugees recounts a story every night until they tell one hundred tales of love and intrigue. Boccaccio offered insight into how these medieval Italians conceived of illness.

Laura de Noves is thought to be the inspiration for Italian poet Petrarch. [Wikimedia]

In the year then of our Lord 1348, there happened at Florence, the finest city in all Italy, a most terrible plague; which, whether owing to the influence of the planets, or that it was sent from God as a just punishment for our sins...

BEYOND INSPIRING POETRY, the plague tested traditional Christian ideas for some and provoked others to become flagellants. These people marched half naked across the European countryside while whipping themselves and fellow marchers bloody in the belief that self-punishment was an answer to the epidemic. Some flagellants used wooden switches,

The plague of Florence, described in Boccaccio's *Decameron*, is depicted here in a later etching. *[Wikimedia]*

thorns, or horsewhips. Many others carried a "scourge"—a type of lash with three tails. As described by one witness in London in 1350, these tails had knots at the end and sometimes had nails fixed in them.

The scenes playing out around medieval Europe were in some ways as horrifying and frightful as the Black Death itself.

A fifteenth-century woodcut depicts flagellants with their scourges.
[Wikimedia]

Whipping themselves bloody, the flagellants would fall on the ground, chanting and stretching their arms in the sign of the cross. Then each man would step over the others and give a stroke of the scourge to the man in front of him.

A great wave of anti-Semitic persecution also swept Europe during the plague years. Many Christians wrongly and unfairly accused Jewish people of poisoning wells. Already banned from most of France by the early 1300s, Jews were accused of being responsible for spreading plague and were burned to death, often after being tortured into false confessions.

While Jewish people became convenient scapegoats to some European Christians, many others began to question religious authority. Doubts about the Church and discontent with its response to the plague helped contribute to a dawning era of inquiry and experiment, flowering in the Renaissance, the Protestant Reformation, and the Enlightenment. By drastically reducing the number of available laborers, the Black Death also helped pave the way for the end of Europe's feudal system. Workers were able to demand better wages and working conditions.

While Western histories tend to focus on the plague in medieval Europe, the Black Death also struck the Islamic world. Born in Tunis, Arab historian Ibn Khaldūn is credited as a pioneering sociologist and demographer, trained in the scholarly traditions of Islam. He recorded the impact of the plague, which took both his parents in 1348, when he was a teenager:

> *Civilization decreased with the decrease of mankind. Cities and buildings were laid waste, roads and way signs were obliterated, settlements and mansions became empty, dynasties and tribes grew weak. . . . When there is a general change of conditions, it is as if the entire creation had changed and*

the whole world had been altered, as if it were a new and
repeated creation, a world brought into existence anew.

FOR IBN KHALDŪN, as well as European Christians, the reason for the plague was unknowable—as it had been for Thucydides in ancient Greece. The idea that microscopic organisms carried disease was simply not imaginable.

The answer came much later. More than five hundred years after the Black Death, it was discovered that fleas living in the fur of rats carried the particular bacteria that caused the plague. These stowaway rats were unwelcome passengers on ships sailing from Asian ports to European cities. So were the fleas hitching rides on the rats. The fleas completed the journey, jumping from rats to human hosts on land, always looking for a warm place. Once bitten by an infected flea, people could spread it to others. Plague was transmitted by human-to-human means or airborne contact—just as the common cold is spread through coughing, sneezing, and hand touching.

The Age of Discovery

ISOLATED FOR CENTURIES by oceans still uncrossed, the American continents were apparently spared many of the plagues and other contagious diseases that afflicted Europe, Africa, and Asia. That protective shield of vast distances would

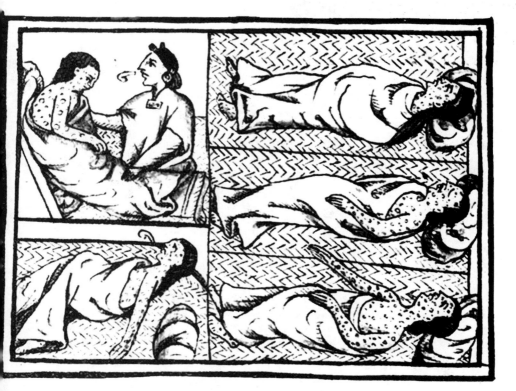

A depiction of Aztec people suffering from smallpox after the arrival of the Spanish. *[Wikimedia]*

Milestones in Medical History

994-1865

994–995 A still-mysterious epidemic wipes out half of the Japanese population.

1347 A pandemic of bubonic and pneumonic plague begins in Europe, killing about a third of the continent's population; the Black Death kills an estimated seventy-five million people worldwide, with a possible death toll of as many as 200 million.

1492 Following Columbus, Europeans carry such diseases as smallpox to the Americas, decimating many native nations.

1495 A previously unknown disease erupts in Europe, first appearing in Naples during a war with France; some call it the Great Pox, but it is widely known as syphilis.

1665–1666 London's Great Plague, a second wave of bubonic plague, kills between seventy-five thousand and a hundred thousand people, about one-fifth of the city's population.

1702 A wave of yellow fever hits New York, killing about 10 percent of the population at the time.

1721–1722 Boston is hit by smallpox, and a handful of doctors experiment with the practice of inoculation.

August 1793 Yellow fever strikes Philadelphia, then the nation's capital, killing about 10 percent of the population at the time, one of the most severe localized epidemics in U.S. history.

1798 British physician Edward Jenner announces his successful experiment with smallpox vaccine made from cowpox virus, a milder form of smallpox.

1817–1823 The first recorded cholera pandemic strikes India. British troops carry the disease to the Middle East, and Arab slave traders carry it to East Africa.

1826–1837 A second cholera pandemic begins in Europe and spreads to the Americas.

1846–1863 A third worldwide cholera pandemic occurs. In the American West, pioneers carry the disease to the Native American population with devastating results.

1854 Florence Nightingale, pioneering British nurse, arrives in Turkey during the Crimean War and introduces key sanitary reforms that reduce the death rate in hospitals.
      During a London cholera epidemic, physician John Snow shows that the disease is spread by contaminated drinking water.

1865 British surgeon Joseph Lister introduces use of carbolic acid in surgery, beginning the use of antiseptics.

be breached with ghastly consequences when the Spanish conquistadores arrived in the Americas. Bringing mass slavery along with horses, guns, and swords never seen by Native American people, the Spanish also carried smallpox and other diseases.

"As the Indians did not know the remedy of the disease . . . they died in heaps, like bedbugs," the Spanish friar Toribio Motolinía later recorded of the smallpox outbreak among the Aztecs. "In many places it happened that everyone in a house died and, as it was impossible to bury the great number of dead, they pulled down the houses over them so that their homes become their tombs."

The precise number of Native Americans living in the Caribbean islands and the Americas when Columbus and his three ships dropped anchor in 1492 is unknown, but many of them would ultimately be wiped out by disease. Across the Caribbean, and in Mexico and Peru, Native American populations fell victim to what are known as "virgin soil epidemics." Coined by historian and geographer Alfred W. Crosby, the term refers to outbreaks "in which the populations at risk have had no previous contact with the diseases that strike them and are therefore immunologically almost defenseless."

WHEN THE MAYFLOWER Pilgrims arrived in Massachusetts in 1620, they found bleached bones—all that was left in a once-thriving Native American settlement. It is now thought that this village had been emptied by a mysterious plague probably carried by European fisherman and traders plying the Atlantic waters and occasionally landing in what is now New England. The Pilgrims settled in this ghostly site and named it Plymouth.

As tens of thousands of English Puritan settlers arrived in Massachusetts and spread across colonial New England in the early 1600s, smallpox and other diseases wiped out entire native nations. "For the natives, they are near all dead of the smallpox," Puritan leader John Winthrop reported in a 1634 letter to London. Believing that God was emptying the land to make way for his Puritan followers, the devout and self-righteous Winthrop wrote, "So the Lord hath cleared our title to what we possess."

By the early 1700s, smallpox still plagued the Americas, and descendants of European settlers lost some of the acquired immunity that had protected their ancestors. In 1721, Boston confronted a full-blown smallpox epidemic, and some doctors had begun to advocate a controversial response called inoculation. Unsavory as it sounds, the practice involved cutting a healthy person's skin and introducing a small amount of pus from an infected smallpox patient.

Besides the incision and introducing the pus, the treatment required a careful diet and regular purges, or vomits stimulated by syrup of ipecac—once widely used to induce vomiting when a person swallowed a poisonous substance. (The American Academy of Pediatrics no longer recommends syrup of ipecac for home use.) The idea behind this procedure was simple: provoke a very mild case of the disease to create immunity against a more dangerous bout.

Inoculation, or variolation, had been used in Asia and Africa for centuries, and its adoption in America is due to an unexpected source. "The idea had come from a slave belonging to Cotton Mather, an African named Onesimus, who had said the practice was long established in Africa, where those with courage to use it were made immune," writes John Adams's biographer David McCullough. "He had his own scar on his arm to show."

The practice was controversial in colonial Massachusetts. Some people believed that it was wrong to tamper with an illness that was part of a divine plan for mankind.

A prominent Puritan minister and judge at the infamous Salem witch trials, Cotton Mather had long advocated for inoculation, which gained some prominent supporters. John Adams had it performed in 1764, and Benjamin Franklin, a scientist as well as printer, was inoculated and became a staunch advocate of the procedure. After the revolution broke out and smallpox was rampaging through Boston in 1776, Abigail Adams and her children were inoculated.

This procedure was an early and less effective version of

what is now called vaccination, pioneered in 1798 by Englishman Edward Jenner. Observing country life, Jenner had been intrigued by the fact that milkmaids exposed to cowpox, a milder form of smallpox, seemed less likely to contract the more deadly disease. Jenner successfully used the cowpox virus to prevent the more dangerous smallpox. The word "vaccination" comes from *vacca*, the Latin word for cow.

From personal experience, George Washington understood that a bout of smallpox provided immunity. In 1751, when he was nineteen years old, George Washington fell gravely ill with smallpox while on the island of Barbados. Two weeks after arriving on the Caribbean island, Washington was running a high fever and had a raging headache. Angry red sores—called pustules, or pocks—began erupting on his face and scalp. Anyone who has suffered a childhood case of chicken pox knows what these itchy, pus-filled sores look like. But George Washington did not have chicken pox. "Was strongly attacked with the small Pox," Washington recorded in his diary on November 17.

That diary entry was his last for more than three weeks. As Washington lay in his sickbed in Barbados, it was touch and go—the young man who would be president had fallen victim to one of history's most lethal killers.

When General George Washington later took command of the American rebel army in 1775, smallpox was already beginning to ravage his troops outside Boston. Often overlooked by American history books, smallpox eventually killed more than one hundred thousand people during the American revolutionary years. Describing this seven-year outbreak of the illness, historian Elizabeth Fenn writes, "With the exception of the war itself, epidemic smallpox was the greatest upheaval to afflict the continent in these years."

As America's president, George Washington witnessed another deadly wave of disease when yellow fever swept over Philadelphia—then America's capital city—in 1793. Yellow fever began with chills, headaches, and other body aches. High fever and constipation followed. Then the victim's skin and eyeballs turned yellow—giving the disease its name. Bleeding from the nose, gums, and intestines preceded vomiting and delirium. Eventually death took about half of yellow fever victims. In Philadelphia, the toll reached more than five thousand, or about 10 percent of the city's population at the time. It was not yet understood that yellow fever was spread by the bite of a certain kind of mosquito.

Modern Age Medical Miracles

UNTIL THE LATE nineteenth century, most physicians and scientists clung to ideas that had originated with Hippocrates and the ancient Greek theories of disease. The most widely shared belief was that epidemics came from putrid-smelling air or fog known as "miasma," a word that comes from the Greek word for pollution. This idea was also expressed in the Italian words *mala aria*—meaning bad air—and the source of the word "malaria." The notion that rotting organic matter in swamps or sewage in dirty streets was the cause of many diseases held sway in the medical world until well into the early twentieth century.

The idea that organisms invisible to the naked eye were the true causes of illness began to take hold following a serious outbreak of cholera in London in August 1854. A horrifying and highly deadly disease, cholera strikes the intestines with violent vomiting and uncontrollable diarrhea, followed by rapid dehydration and death. Cholera arrived in Europe in the early nineteenth century, traveling from the Ganges Delta in India, when British troops serving there carried it back to England.

As more Londoners fell victim to cholera's deadly curse, physician John Snow had a theory. A pioneer in the use of ether and chloroform to put patients to sleep during surgery, Snow set out on some medical sleuthing. To track the outbreak, he carefully charted cholera's spread in the crowded Golden Square district in London, where the outbreak was most

Milestones in Medical History

1876–78 The germ theory of disease begins to transform the medical world after German biologist Robert Koch confirms that bacteria causes anthrax, a disease of cattle and sheep that also infects humans. Soon after, Frenchman Louis Pasteur presents his research paper "Germ Theory and Its Applications to Medicine and Surgery."

1882 Koch identifies the bacteria that causes tuberculosis, perhaps the most widespread infectious disease in the world at the time.

1885 Pasteur inoculates the first human patient against rabies.

1889 The worst influenza pandemic recorded to this time begins in Asia or Siberia, eventually spreading globally.

1894 The bacteria that causes plague is identified, and a few years later, the role of fleas and rats in carrying the disease is discovered.

1895 The x-ray is discovered by Wilhelm Röntgen, and x-ray machines are soon being used to diagnose diseases and aid surgery.

1899 The German company Bayer introduces aspirin as a pain reliever.

1900 The U.S. Army Yellow Fever Commission frees Cuba of yellow fever by eradicating breeding sites of mosquitoes.

In the nineteenth and early twentieth centuries, cholera and other
diseases were believed to be spread by "bad air," or miasma.
This is a representation of a cholera outbreak from 1831.
[National Library of Medicine]

deadly. Like the fictional Sherlock Holmes, Snow was a bril-
liant detective and identified the central point of the cholera
outbreak—what might be called "ground zero" today. He
demonstrated that the source of the disease was not miasma,
the foggy, bad air from London's industrial smokestacks and
rotting garbage, but a water pump contaminated by human
waste.

A diaper worn by a sick six-month-old girl suffering from cholera had been soaked in a bucket of warm water. The water was then tossed into a cesspool—a common ditch where waste and sewage were thrown before modern sanitary systems existed. The tainted water from that cesspool eventually found its way into the well and the Broad Street pump shared by residents of the neighborhood. Cholera quickly spread throughout the London neighborhood. Snow had the pump handle removed, and the cholera subsided.

Even though the precise organism—later identified as the cholera bacteria—was still unknown, Snow had scored an enormous victory for science over superstition by providing clear evidence that the disease was carried in contaminated water. Cities like London soon began to implement his practical solution to cholera and other waterborne diseases—keeping sewage away from drinking water.

Not long after Snow's pioneering detective work, other scientists and doctors began to argue that diseases were carried by microscopic organisms found in water and food, shared by human contact or carried by insects, including mosquitoes. The idea was pioneered in the late nineteenth century by German Robert Koch and Frenchman Louis Pasteur, who used microscopes to revolutionize medicine and establish their "germ theory" of disease.

Early types of magnifying lenses had been used in Europe

The Broad Street Pump—its handle symbolically removed—is a memorial to John Snow for his discovery that a cholera outbreak in London was due to contaminated water from the pump. *[Wikimedia]*

for centuries. During the 1660s, Dutch cloth merchant Antoni van Leeuwenhoek was grinding glass to improve magnifying lenses to better examine the weave of fabrics. Using one of these lenses, Leeuwenhoek looked at pond water and saw what he called "wretched beasties." Leeuwenhoek had seen algae and bacteria, the invisible living organisms that would later be called microbes.

Leeuwenhoek's discovery was largely ignored. "For almost two centuries, the knowledge that the world teemed with small organisms was regarded as an interesting but rather irrelevant fact," medical writer Kathryn Senior explains. "It was a long time before people worked out that bacteria could be a factor in causing some of the diseases that passed from one person to another."

In 1883, Robert Koch proved John Snow correct when he identified the "cholera bacillus" present in the intestines and feces of infected patients. The same bacteria were sometimes present in drinking water. Around the same time, France's Louis Pasteur had become famous for proving that heating milk could prevent it from souring and spoiling. His name lives on in the word "pasteurization," which made milk much safer by killing the bacteria.

Pasteur made another great medical leap by creating a vaccine for anthrax—another killer disease that infects both livestock and humans. In 1881, he successfully showed that heating the bacteria could reduce its power to infect. He injected animals with his anthrax vaccine in a daring public experiment in which the vaccinated animals all survived while "unprotected" animals that had not received the vaccine all died.

Robert Koch's discoveries also played a role in one of the most notorious and still controversial disease outbreaks in American history. In 1902, Koch announced that bacteria present in human feces caused typhoid fever. He had also found that people could have these germs but not get sick—he called them "healthy carriers." Infected people who failed to wash their hands after using the toilet and then prepared food could pass along the disease—even though they showed no signs of being sick.

In 1906, there was an outbreak of typhoid fever in the New York City area. The source of the outbreak was tracked to a woman named Mary Mallon, an Irish immigrant working as a cook. When she refused to have her urine and stool tested, and then ran away, the New York Health Department had Mary Mallon arrested and forcibly tested. Her samples were teeming with bacteria, even though Mary appeared to be in good health. In 1907, without being tried for any crime, she was quarantined by the New York Department of Health in a cottage on North Brother Island in the East River.

She successfully sued for her release, and in 1909 newspapers identified Mary Mallon as Typhoid Mary, and called her

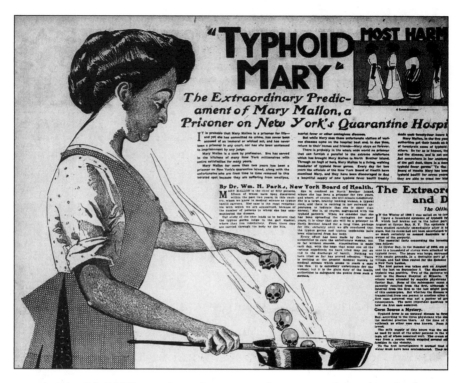

A June 20, 1909, article in the *New York American* first identified
Mary Mallon as "Typhoid Mary." *[Wikimedia]*

"the most dangerous woman in America." A judge permitted
her release with the promise she would not work as a cook.

But she did. Using the name "Mary Brown," she worked as
a cook at a maternity hospital where typhoid fever then broke
out; at least 25 doctors, nurses, staff, and a patient fell ill, and
two died. On March 26, 1915, Mary Mallon was arrested
again—"screaming and cursing them for persecution," notes
science writer Deborah Blum.

Mary Mallon was returned to the island quarantine, where she spent the rest of her life. In 1918, a doctor on the island gave her a job as a medical assistant. With official permission, she was later free to make visits off the island and never tried to escape. Mary Mallon suffered a stroke in 1932 and spent the next six years as a patient in the hospital until her death in 1938. Her case is still debated whenever governments and health officials deal with forcibly quarantining a potentially sick person who may pose a danger to the public health.

The work of men like Pasteur and Koch had created an astonishing medical revolution. "With the growing and profound knowledge that many diseases are caused by microscopic organisms and that the spread of disease can be prevented, the Western world was transformed," Gina Kolata writes. "The results were dramatic. In large areas of the world, many of the killer diseases seemed tamed, or even vanquished, and deadly epidemics seemed to be relics of the past."

Even with the successful discovery of mosquitoes as the cause of yellow fever, and despite the advances made by "microbe hunters" like Pasteur, Koch, and Paul Ehrlich—the German physician and scientist who created a cure for syphilis—many doctors and scientists resisted germ theory. They persisted in the belief that deadly diseases hung in smoke, fog, and even household dust.

This cartoon from *Puck* magazine shows the fear that contagious diseases might be shaken loose in household dust.

[U.S. National Library of Medicine]

The pace of medical discoveries continued after the Spanish flu epidemic. In 1928, the Scottish biologist Alexander Fleming noticed that one of his bacteria dishes was contaminated with a common bread and fruit mold. It looked like the mold had secreted something that was inhibiting the growth of the bacteria. He named this "mold juice" penicillin. Introducing the age of antibiotics, penicillin revolutionized medicine and health care.

Milestones in Medical History

1902-1916

December 1902 The International Sanitary Bureau, today's Pan American Health Organization, is established as the world's first permanent international health organization.

1907–1910 In New York, an outbreak of typhoid fever is traced to Irish immigrant Mary Mallon, a cook who infected at least twenty-two people, one of whom died. Mallon is forced into quarantine. Although identified as Typhoid Mary in the press, she is released in 1910 on the promise that she never work as a cook again.

March 27, 1915 Following outbreaks of typhoid fever in New Jersey and Manhattan, where Mary Mallon had worked again as a cook, she is returned to quarantine. She will remain there for the rest of her life, dying in 1938. Fifty-one cases of typhoid, and three deaths, would be directly attributed to her.

July 1916 The first large-scale polio epidemic hits the United States.

1918-2016

March 1918 The first cases of Spanish influenza appear among army recruits in Kansas. Within months, every continent and country is affected.

September A second, more deadly, wave of Spanish flu strikes the United States, with the first reported outbreak in the Boston area.

1922 The Health Section of the League of Nations is founded. It is the forerunner of the World Health Organization.

1928 Penicillin is discovered.

1932 The infamous Tuskegee Study of Untreated Syphilis in the Negro Male begins, using poor African American men in Alabama who are only told they are being treated for "bad blood." For forty years, the Public Health Service fails to provide these men with proper treatment, including penicillin. The study is finally exposed in 1972.

1941 The first flu vaccines are produced.

1944 A new antibiotic drug, streptomycin, cures a tuberculosis patient. With this and other similar medicines, many infectious diseases are effectively eliminated in the developed world. Over time, however, many bacteria begin to develop resistance to these widely used antibiotics.

1946 The World Health Organization is formed by sixty-one countries in New York; it begins operations two years later.

Born out of the wartime mission to control malaria, the CDC opens its doors as the Communicable Disease Center in a small building in Atlanta. Its primary original mission is to prevent malaria from spreading across the nation.

1955 The Salk polio vaccine is introduced after massive testing of schoolchildren. Polio is largely conquered in the developed world.

1957–1958 A global pandemic of Asian flu strikes, causing one to two million deaths, relatively mild compared to the pandemic of 1918.

1959 A clinic in the Belgian Congo takes a blood sample from an ill Bantu man. Analysis decades later finds that it contains human immunodeficiency virus. This is now considered the first recorded AIDS case.

1975 In Lyme, Connecticut, doctors identify the first cases of Lyme disease, which is carried by small deer ticks.

1976 A deadly form of pneumonia strikes American Legionnaires returning from a state convention in Philadelphia. After six months, the Legionnaires' disease is attributed to bacteria in a hotel's air-conditioning system.

1977 The last case of naturally occurring smallpox is recorded after a global vaccination campaign. Under a 1979 agreement, the world's remaining stock of smallpox virus is stored in two laboratories, one in Russia and one at the CDC in Atlanta.

1981 The Centers for Disease Control and Prevention reports that hundreds of gay men are suffering from rare ailments associated with weakened immune systems. Eventually it will be known as AIDS, acquired immune deficiency syndrome.

1983 The virus that causes AIDS is isolated and named HIV, human immunodeficiency virus.

1986 Mad cow disease is discovered among cattle in Britain. It is eventually passed to humans, causing brain damage and death.

1995 A new class of anti-HIV drugs sharply reduce the death toll from HIV and AIDS

More than three hundred people die in Zaire from Ebola virus, which first appeared in 1976 in two simultaneous outbreaks. One was in South Sudan and the other in the Democratic Republic of Congo, in a village near the Ebola River, from which the disease takes its name.

1997 An outbreak of avian, or bird, flu strikes Hong Kong. The city destroys 1.5 million farm birds to control the spread of the infection.

2002—2004 A new viral disease called SARS, severe acute respiratory syndrome, spreads from South China around the world. An aggressive global response contains the outbreak, although eighty-five hundred are infected and eight hundred people die.

2014 The largest outbreak of Ebola virus since 1976 begins in West Africa.

2015—2016 A widespread epidemic of the mosquito-borne Zika virus strikes Brazil and spreads to other parts of the Americas.

APPENDIX 2

PREVENTING THE FLU: ADVICE FROM THE CDC

THE CENTERS FOR Disease Control and Prevention (cdc .gov) offers a great deal of information about the flu, how to prevent it, and what to do if you get it. First, it recommends an annual flu vaccine as the most important step. The flu virus mutates, and each year the vaccines change to address the new strains.

The CDC also offers a list of everyday actions to take to prevent the spread of germs:

- Try to avoid close contact with sick people.

- While sick, limit contact with others as much as possible to keep from infecting them.

- If you are sick with flu symptoms, stay home for at least twenty-four hours after your fever is gone, except to get medical care or other necessities. (Your fever should be gone for twenty-four hours without the use of a fever-reducing medicine.)

- Cover your nose and mouth with a tissue when you cough or sneeze. Throw the tissue in the trash after you use it.

- Wash your hands often with soap and water. If soap and water are not available, use an alcohol-based hand sanitizer.

- Avoid touching your eyes, nose, and mouth. Germs spread this way.

- Clean and disinfect surfaces and objects that may be contaminated with germs.

BIBLIOGRAPHY

BOOKS ABOUT FLU AND DISEASE

Allen, Arthur. *Vaccine: The Controversial Story of Medicine's Greatest Lifesaver*. New York: Norton, 2007.

Barry, John M. *The Great Influenza: The Story of the Deadliest Pandemic in History*. New York: Penguin Books, 2004.

Cantor, Norman F. *In the Wake of the Plague: The Black Death and the World It Made*. New York: Free Press, 2001.

Collier, Richard. *The Plague of the Spanish Lady: The Influenza Pandemic of 1918–1919*. London: Allison & Busby, 1996.

Crosby, Alfred W. *America's Forgotten Pandemic: The Influenza of 1918*. Cambridge, United Kingdom: Cambridge University Press, 2003.

Davies, Pete. *The Devil's Flu: The World's Deadliest Influenza Epidemic and the Scientific Hunt for the Virus That Caused It*. New York: Holt, 2000.

de Kruif, Paul. *Microbe Hunters*. New York: Harvest Books, 1996.

Diamond, Jared. *Guns, Germs, and Steel: The Fates of Human Societies*. New York: Norton, 1998.

Dobson, Mary. *The Story of Medicine: From Bloodletting to Biotechnology*. New York: Quercus, 2013.

Fenn, Elizabeth A. *Pox Americana: The Great Smallpox Epidemic of 1775–82*. New York: Hill & Wang, 2001.

France, David. *How to Survive a Plague: The Inside Story of How Citizens and Science Tamed AIDS*. New York: Knopf, 2016.

Honigsbaum, Mark. *Living with Enza: The Forgotten Story of Great Britain and the Great Flu Pandemic of 1918*. New York: Palgrave Macmillan, 2009.

Jarrow, Gail. *Bubonic Plague: When Plague Invaded America*. Honesdale, Pa.: Calkins Creek, 2016.

———. *Fatal Fever: Tracking Down Typhoid Mary*. Honesdale, Pa.: Calkins Creek, 2015.

Johnson, Steven. *The Ghost Map: The Story of London's Most Terrifying Epidemic—And How It Changed Science, Cities, and the Modern World*. New York: Riverhead Books, 2006.

Kolata, Gina. *Flu: The Story of the Great Influenza Pandemic of 1918 and the Search for the Virus That Caused It*. New York: Simon & Schuster, 1999.

Leavitt, Judith Walzer. *Typhoid Mary: Captive to the Public's Health*. Boston: Beacon Press, 1996.

Magner, Lois N. *A History of Medicine*. New York: Marcel Dekker, 1992.

Murphy, Jim. *An American Plague: The True and Terrifying Story of the Yellow Fever Epidemic of 1793*. New York: Clarion, 2003.

Quammen, David. *Spillover: Animal Infections and the Next Human Pandemic*. New York: Norton, 2012.

Shah, Sonia. *Pandemic: Tracking Contagions, from Cholera to Ebola and Beyond*. New York: Farrar, Straus and Giroux, 2016.

Timberg, Craig, and Daniel Halperin. *Tinderbox: How the West Sparked the AIDS Epidemic and How the World Can Finally Overcome It*. New York: Penguin Press, 2012.

Youngerman, Barry. *Pandemics and Global Health*. New York: Facts on File, 2008.

BOOKS ABOUT WORLD WAR I

Axelrod, Alan. *Selling the Great War: The Making of American Propaganda.* New York: Palgrave Macmillan, 2009.

Berg, A. Scott. *Wilson.* New York: Putnam, 2013.

Berg, A. Scott, ed. *World War I and America: Told by the Americans Who Lived It.* New York: Library of America, 2017.

Brittain, Vera. *Testament of Youth.* New York: Penguin Books, 2005.

Cooper, John Milton, Jr. *Woodrow Wilson: A Biography.* New York: Knopf, 2009.

Cowsill, Alan. *World War One: 1914–1918.* New Delhi, India: Campfire, 2014.

Freedman, Russell. *The War to End All Wars: World War I.* Boston: Clarion Books, 2010.

Hart, Peter. *The Somme: The Darkest Hour on the Western Front.* New York: Pegasus Books, 2008.

Hastings, Max. *Catastrophe 1914: Europe Goes to War.* New York: Knopf, 2013.

Hochschild, Adam. *To End All Wars: A Story of Loyalty and Rebellion, 1914–1918.* Boston: Houghton Mifflin, 2011.

Jünger, Ernst. *Storm of Steel.* Translated by Michael Hofmann. New York: Penguin Books, 2016.

Keegan, John. *The First World War.* New York: Knopf, 1999.

Larson, Erik. *Dead Wake: The Last Crossing of the* Lusitania. New York: Crown, 2015.

MacMillan, Margaret. *Paris 1919: Six Months That Changed the World.* New York: Random House, 2001.

Philpott, William. *War of Attrition: Fighting the First World War.* New York: Overlook Press, 2014.

Rubin, Richard. *The Last of the Doughboys: The Forgotten Generation and Their Forgotten World War.* Boston: Houghton Mifflin Harcourt, 2013.

Tuchman, Barbara W. *The Guns of August.* New York: Ballantine, 1994.

Winter, J. M. *The Experience of World War I.* New York: Oxford University Press, 1989.

OTHER REFERENCES AND SOURCE MATERIALS

Gabler, Neal. *Walt Disney: The Triumph of the American Imagination.* New York: Knopf, 2006.

Givner, Joan. *Katherine Anne Porter: A Life.* Athens, Ga.: University of Georgia Press, 1991.

Gwenda Blair. *The Trumps: Three Generations of Builders and a Presidential Candidate.* New York: Simon & Schuster, 2000.

Hemingway, Ernest. *A Farewell to Arms.* New York: Scribner, 2014.

Hersey, John. *Hiroshima.* New York: Vintage, 1989.

McCullough, David. *The Path Between the Seas: The Creation of the Panama Canal 1870–1914.* New York: Simon & Schuster, 1977.

Porter, Katherine Anne. *Pale Horse, Pale Rider: Three Short Novels.* New York: Modern Library, 1998.

Remarque, Erich Maria. *All Quiet on the Western Front: The Illustrated Edition.* Translated by A. W. Wheen. Boston: Bulfinch Press, 1996.

Wolfe, Thomas. *Look Homeward, Angel.* New York: Scribner, 2006.

NOTES

INTRODUCTION

6   "It was impossible to estimate": Mrs. Nichols, "Report of the Expedition," July 21, 1919, National Archives, in John M. Barry, *The Great Influenza*, pp. 360–361.

6   an estimated 675,000 Americans: Crosby, *America's Forgotten Pandemic*, p. 206.

6   more Americans died from the flu: Kolata, *Flu*, p. x.

7   the Spanish flu killed as many Americans: "Statistics Overview: HIV Surveillance," *HIV Surveillance Report: Diagnoses of HIV Infection in the United States and Dependent Areas*, Centers for Disease Control and Prevention (Updated May 18, 2017), cdc.gov/hiv/statistics/overview/index.html.

10   The Black Death killed: "The Five Deadliest Outbreaks and Pandemics in History," Culture of Health Blog, Robert Wood Johnson Foundation, December 16, 2013, rwjf.org/en/culture-of-health/2013/12/the_five_dead liesto.html.

10   one person in twenty alive in 1918: Barry Youngerman, *Pandemics and Global Health*, p. 96.

11   "Children lost fathers": Margaret MacMillan, *Paris 1919* , p. xxvi.

13   "The flu was expunged from newspapers": Kolata, *Flu*, p. 53.

13   "The average college graduate": Alfred Crosby, *America's Forgotten Pandemic*, pp. 314–315.

14   the Naples Soldier: Niall Johnson, *Britain and the 1918–19 Influenza Pandemic: A Dark Epilogue* (London: Routledge, 2006), p. 160.

14   The Russians called it: Szymon Słomczyński, "There are sick people everywhere," rdsg-ihpan.edu.pl/images/RDSGpdfy/2012/RDSG_2012_05-Slomczynski.pdf.

14   Soldiers fighting in the Great War: Kolata, *Flu*, p. 11.

16   The word is thought to come from: Kolata, p. 6.

CHAPTER ONE

21   I gather that the epidemic of grippe: Harvey Cushing, *From a Surgeon's Journal 1915–1918* (Boston: Little, Brown, 1936), p. 389, quoted in Barry, *The Great Influenza*, p. 171.

26   Convincing his mother to sign: Neal Gabler, *Walt Disney*, p. 37.

29   But active service: Jean Edward Smith, *FDR*, pp. 158–159.

33   "Why . . . entangle our peace": George Washington, "Farewell Address (1796)," Avalon Project, Yale Law School, avalon.law.yale.edu/18th_century/washing.asp. Accessed July 8, 2017.

33   "the organization and mobilization": Woodrow Wilson, "Address to Congress Requesting a Declaration of War Against Germany," April 2, 1917, Presidential Speeches, Miller Center, millercenter.org/the-presidency.

35   "military boomtowns of tents and barracks": Allan R. Millett, Peter Maslowski, and William B. Feis, *For the Common Defense: A Military History of the United States from 1607 to 2012* (New York: Free Press, 2012), p. 355.

36   in the morning of March 4: Kolata, *Flu*, p. 10.

36   The medical officer who examined him: M. Honingsbaum, *Living with Enza*, pp. 42–43.

43   But they are mostly spread: "How Flu Spreads," Centers for Disease Control and Prevention, cdc.gov/flu/about/disease/spread.htm.

44   "It starts at the back of the throat": Jason Socrates Bardi, "The Gross Science of a Cough and Sneeze," *Live Science*, June 14, 2009, livescience.com/3686-gross-science-cough-sneeze.html.

44   "knock-me-down fever": Crosby, *America's Forgotten Pandemic*, p. 19.

45   "Today such news": Crosby, p. 19

46   In the midst of a war: Collier, *The Plague of the Spanish Lady*, p. 8.

46   "I gather that the epidemic of grippe": Cushing quoted in Barry, *The Great Influenza*, p. 171.

47   Half a million of General Ludendorff's soldiers: Crosby, p. 26

47   the British army optimistically declared that the epidemic was over: Barry, p. 182.

CHAPTER TWO

49   It is horrible: Roy to Burt, September 29, 1918, in N. R. Grist, "Pandemic Influenza 1918," *British Medical Journal*, no. 6205 (1979), in Kolata, *Flu*, p. 14. bmj.com/content/bmj/2/6205/1632.full.pdf.

49   In the morning the dead bodies: Victor C. Vaughan, *A Doctor's Memories* (Indianapolis: Bobbs-Merrill, 1926), p. 384, quoted in Barry, p. 190. archive.org/details/doctorsmemories013852mbp.

49   "They looked larger than ordinary men": Vera Brittain, *Testament of Youth*, pp. 420–421.

50   "They very rapidly develop": Roy to Burt, September 29, 1918, in Kolata, *Flu*, p. 14.

50   "A considerable number of American negroes": "Epidemic Guard for Port," *New York Times*, August 19, 1918, quoted in Barry, *The Great Influenza*, p. 182.

51   A STRANGE FORM OF DISEASE: Richard Collier, *The Plague of the Spanish Lady*, p. 7.

51   Millions had fallen ill: Collier, p. 11.

51   some men were transferred to the U.S. Naval Hospital: Crosby, *America's Forgotten Pandemic*, p. 39.

52   "Fevers ran from 101°": Crosby, p. 39.

54   front pages of newspapers: John F. Kelly, "Autumn 1918: Washington's Season of Death," *Washington Post*, February 1, 2004.

56   rumors of German treachery: Kolata, *Flu*, p. 4.

58   the Spanish flu had struck: Kolata, p. 15.

59   "They are placed on the cots": Vaughan, *A Doctor's Memories*, pp. 383–384, in Barry, *The Great Influenza*, p. 189.

59   Built by the largest labor force: "History," Fort Devens Museum, fortdevensmuseum.org.

61   "In the morning the dead bodies": Vaughan, p. 384, in Barry, p. 190, archive.org/details/doctorsmemories 013852mbp.

61   "This must be some new kind of infection": Rufus Cole to Simon Flexner, May 26, 1936, *Influenza Encyclopedia*, University of Michigan Library, hdl.handle.net/2027/spo.1570flu.0015.751. Accessed July 9, 2017.

63   fifty thousand people in Massachusetts: Kolata, *Flu*, p. 18.

63   "New men will almost surely contract the disease": Charles Richard to Army Adjutant General, September 25, 1918, quoted in Barry, p. 302. history.amedd.army.mil/booksdocs/wwi/1918flu/History/sanitationUSCh16 .htm.

63   "The deaths at Camp Devens": Charles Richard to Army Chief of Staff, September 26, 1918, quoted in Barry, p. 302. history.amedd.army.mil/booksdocs/wwi/1918flu/History/sanitationUSCh16.htm.

63   "I was on duty at Great Lakes": Jay McAuliffe, "James H. Wallace," War Stories, *Pandemic Influenza Storybook*, April 9, 2013, Centers for Disease Control and Prevention, cdc.gov/publications/panflu/.

64   "Each incident": Kolata, *Flu*, p. 18

CHAPTER THREE

67   IF YOU MUST KISS: "If You Must Kiss, Kiss Via Kerchief, Is Warning," *The New York Sun*, August 17, 1918. chronicling america.loc.gov/lccn/sn83030431/1918-08-17/ed-1/seq-12/. Accessed July 9, 2017.

67   On St. Mark's Place in Manhattan's East Village: Youngerman, *Pandemics and Global Health*, p. xi. Barry Youngerman is Rose's nephew.

69   So did a German immigrant: Lawrence Downes, "Donald Trump: An American Tale," *Taking Note* (blog), *New York Times*, June 30, 2015, takingnote.blogs.nytimes.com/2015/06/30/.

69   He later returned to New York: Gwenda Blair, *The Trumps*, pp. 116–117.

71   According to Salvation Army tradition: "The History of Donut Day," The Salvation Army Metropolitan Division. centralusa.salvationarmy.org/metro/donutdayhistory/. Accessed July 9, 2017.

72   The nickname "doughboy": Michael E. Hanlon, "The Origins of Doughboy," worldwar1.com/dbc/origindb.htm. Accessed July 9, 2017.

73   During America's two years of preparation: Millet, Maslowski, and Feis, For the Common Defense, p. 352.

74   A volunteer group called: Barry, The Great Influenza, p. 124.

77   The health commissioner advised: New York Sun, August 17, 1918, chroniclingamerica.loc.gov/lccn/sn83030431/1918-08-17/ed-1/seq-12/. Accessed July 9, 2017.

77   When twenty-five people: "City Is Not in Danger from Spanish Grip," New York Times, September 13, 2017. Accessed July 9, 2017.

78   "They're as blue as huckleberries": Collier, p. 39.

78   more than twenty thousand deaths in New York City: Blum, The Poisoner's Handbook, p. 43. Also "The 1918 Influenza Epidemic in New York City: A Review of the Public Health Reports," Public Health Reports 2010, US National Library of Medicine, ncbi.nlm.nih.gov/pmc/articles/PMC2862336/. Accessed July 9, 2017.

78   The "filthy habit"—spitting in public—was made illegal: "Drastic Steps Taken to Fight Influenza Here," New York Times, October 5, 1918, quoted in Francesco Aimone, "The 1918 Influenza Epidemic in New York City: A Review of the Public Health Response," Public Health Reports 125, suppl. 3 (2010): p. 71–79, ncbi.nlm.nih.gov/pmc/articles/PMC2862336/.

79   "New York is a great cosmopolitan city": "Drastic Steps Taken," quoted in Aimone, "The 1918 Influenza Epidemic in New York."

79   "It got to the place where I would only see patients twice": Deborah Blum, The Poisoner's Handbook: Murder and the Birth of Forensic Medicine in Jazz Age New York (New York: Penguin, 2010), p. 44.

79   New York would see more than thirty thousand deaths: Annual Report of Department of Health of the City of New York, 1918 (New York: William Bratler, 1919), quoted in Aimone, "The 1918 Influenza Epidemic in New York."

79   No person shall appear: Bradford Luckingham, Epidemic in the Southwest (El Paso, Texas: Texas Western Press, 1984), p. 34, quoted in Kolata, p. 23.

81   "Fifty-one Mexican men": Kolata, Flu, p. 25.

81   In Alliance, Nebraska, the Red Cloud family: Vanessa Short Bull, "Sadie Afraid of His Horses–Janis," Finding a Cure, Pandemic Influenza Storybook, April 9, 2013, Centers for Disease Control and Prevention, cdc.gov/publications/panflu/.

83   "His secret weapon": Margarita Pancake, "Elmer 'Bud' Pancake," Finding a Cure, Pandemic Influenza Storybook, April 9, 2013, Centers for Disease Control and Prevention, cdc.gov/publications/panflu/.

84   "If it was difficult to control crowding": Carol R. Byerly, "The U.S. Military and the Influenza Pandemic of 1918-1919," Public Health Reports, U.S. National Library of Medicine 2010, ncbi.nlm.nih.gov/pmc/articles/PMC2862337/.

84   "Influenza exists in epidemic form": John Pershing to Army Adjutant General, cable no. 1744, October 3, 1918, quoted in Kolata, Flu, p. 51.

85   Army Provost Marshal General: Kolata, Flu, p. 18.

85   "The transports became floating caskets": Barry, The Great Influenza, p. 306.

CHAPTER FOUR

89   "I wish those people": Brittain, Testament of Youth, p. 395.

89   "Louder and louder grew the sound": Adam Hochschild, To End All Wars, p. 110.

92   "We are insensible, dead men": Erich Maria Remarque, All Quiet on the Western Front, p. 87.

93   "It was the largest mass movement": Hochschild, To End All Wars, p. 94.

94   The war was principally declared: Hochschild, p. 75.

96   "You will be home": Hochschild, p. 102.

97   "We had bonded together": Jünger, *Storm of Steel*, p. 5.

98   "In a single day": Russell Freedman, *The War to End All Wars*, p. 35.

98   "Opposite was the Church of St. Pierre": Richard Harding Davis, "Horrors of Louvain Told by Eyewitness; Circled Burning City," *New York Tribune*, August 31, 1914. *Chronicling America: Historic American Newspapers.* Library of Congress.

100 "Germany's resources were simply insufficient": Max Hastings, *Catastrophe 1914*, p. 284.

102 "They were mowed down": Freedman, p. 42.

105 "Even today": Hochschild, p. 81.

110 "Were I to advise": Joseph P. Tumulty, *Woodrow Wilson as I Know Him* (Garden City, New York: Doubleday, 1921), p. 233, in Erik Larson, *Dead Wake*, p. 329.

CHAPTER FIVE

117 The sound of artillery: Adam Hochschild, *To End All Wars*, p. 317.

117 Paris also came under bombardment: Adam Hochschild, *To End All Wars*, p. 320.

119 "Because diseases have been the biggest killers": Jared Diamond, *Guns, Germs, and Steel*, p. 197.

119 Leading the commission: "History of the U.S. Army Yellow Fever Commission in Cuba," University of Virginia Health System. exhibits.hsl.virginia.edu/yellowfever/u-s-occupation-cuba/. Accessed July 10, 2017.

121 Without telling his colleagues: John R. Pierce, "James Lazear and Self-Experimentation," Roundtable Discussion on Yellow Fever, September 13, 2005, *The Great Fever*, American Experience, pbs.org/wgbh//amex/fever/sfeature/.

122 In his final delirium: David McCullough, *The Path Between the Seas*, p. 414.

122 "Of all the silly and nonsensical": *Washington Post* editorial, November 2, 1900, in Jim Murphy, *An American Plague*, p. 132.

124 pneumonia triggers the immune system: "Pneumonia: Overview," Mayo Clinic, mayoclinic.org/diseases-conditions/pneumonia/home/ovc-20204676.

124 "an extraordinarily complex, intricate": Barry, *The Great Influenza*, p.107.

126 "We lost lots of them": Lori Woodson, "Pandemic," *Manhattan Mercury*, March 1, 1998, www2.okstate.edu/ww1hist/flu.html.

126 "Most everybody over the country": *Santa Fe Monitor*, February 21, 1918, in Barry, p. 95.

127 "as suddenly as if they had been shot": Barry, p. 93.

127 Although it is not certain: Barry, p. 169.

128 "The timing of the Funston explosion": Barry, p. 97.

129 Public Health Service doctors: Kolata, *Flu*, p. 10.

129 When the United States entered the war: Barry, p. 139.

131 When the war began, there were 403 women: "Military Nurses in World War I," Women in Military Service to America Memorial Foundation, chnm.gmu.edu/courses/rr/s01/cw/students/leeann/historyandcollections/history/lrnmrewwinurses.html.

131 At the end of May: Edwin O. Jordan, *Epidemic Influenza* (Chicago: American Medical Association, 1927), pp. 78–79, quod.lib.umich.edu/cgi/t/text/idx/f/flu/8580flu.0016.858/40/. Accessed July 10, 2017.

132 In June, three thousand men: Collier, *The Plague of the Spanish Lady*, p. 8.

133 The king's doctor said: Collier, p. 20.

134 Paul Ehrlich discovered: Barry, p. 146.

135 "It had only gone underground": Barry, p. 175.

CHAPTER SIX

137 "Obey the laws": Molly J. Billings, "The Public Health Response," *The Influenza Pandemic of 1918*, June 1997, virus.stanford.edu/uda/fluresponse.html.

139 fifty base hospitals: John Barry, *The Great Influenza*, p. 129.

139 According to Red Cross records . . . overseas: "Work in the United States," in *A Statement of Finances and Accomplishments for the Period July 1, 1917 to February 28, 1919* (Washington, D.C.: American Red Cross, 1919), on Medical Front WWI, vlib.us/medical/.

141 "Your country needs every penny": "United States Government War-Savings Stamps: What They Are and Why You Should Buy Them," Washington: Government Printing Office, 1917, p. 3.

142 Some athletes, including Olympic marathoners: Esther Inglis-Arkell, "Rat Poison Strychnine Was an Early Performance-Enhancing Drug," June 11, 2013, Gizmodo iO9, io9.gizmodo.com/why-strychnine-was-an-early -performance-enhancing-drug-512532345.

142 "Miraculously, it worked": Joan Givner, *Katherine Anne Porter: A Life*, p. 126.

142 She had lost all her hair: Joan Givner, *Katherine Anne Porter: A Life*, p. 130.

143 "The two men slid off the desk, leaving": Porter, *Pale Horse, Pale Rider*, p. 184.

143 Four Minute Men: Alan Axelrod, *Selling the Great War: The Making of American Propaganda*, p. 94.

144 original movies: Alan Axelrod, *Selling the Great War: The Making of American Propaganda*, p. 93.

144 "utter, print, write or publish any disloyal": Sedition Act, May 16, 1918, *United States Statutes at Large* 40 (April 1917–March 1919), p. 553, loc.gov/law/help/statutes-at-large/65th-congress/c65.pdf.

145 "I am Public Opinion": Liberty Bond poster described in Barry, *The Great Influenza*, p. 127.

145 "Wilson hated to see the loss": A. Scott Berg, *Wilson*, p. 456.

145 Berlin, Iowa, changed its name to Lincoln: Berg, *Wilson*, p. 456.

145 "American brewers": Crosby, *America's Forgotten Pandemic*, p. 46.

148 "They would do this for several hours a day": Paul Kendall, "Dr. Frank Biberstein," Plantings, *Pandemic Influenza Storybook*, April 9, 2013, Centers for Disease Control and Prevention, cdc.gov/publications/panflu/.

148 Also filling the void was Philadelphia's: James F. Armstrong, "Philadelphia, Nurses, and the Spanish Influenza Pandemic of 1918," *Navy Medicine* 92, no. 2 (March–April 2001): p. 16–20, history.navy.mil/research/library /online-reading-room/title-list-alphabetically/i/influenza/philadelphia-nurses-and-the-spanish-influenza -pandemic-of-1918.html.

148 "Visiting nurses often walked into": Crosby, p. 76.

150 "when no hospital beds were to be had": Mary McCarthy, *Memories of a Catholic Girlhood* (San Diego: Harcourt, 1957), p. 35.

150 "We were beaten all the time": McCarthy, *Memories of a Catholic Girlhood*, p. 64.

151 The health commissioner of New York estimated: Barry, *The Great Influenza*, p. 391.

151 "For Lillian Kancianich": Lillian Kancianich, interview, August 8, 2003, in Nancy K. Bristow, " 'It's as Bad as Anything Can Be': Patients, Identity, and the Influenza Pandemic," *Public Health Reports* 125, suppl. 3 (2010): p. 134–144, ncbi.nlm.nih.gov/pmc/articles/PMC2862342/.

154 "If influenza could have been smothered": Crosby, *America's Forgotten Pandemic*, p. 49.

154 "Racism and legalized segregation": Vanessa Northington Gamble, " 'There Wasn't a Lot of Comforts in Those Days': African Americans, Public Health, and the 1918 Influenza Epidemic," *Public Health Reports* 125, suppl. 3 (2010): p. 114–122, ncbi.nlm.nih.gov/pmc/articles/PMC2862340/.

155 In Philadelphia, there were two black hospitals: Gamble, " 'There Wasn't a Lot of Comforts in Those Days,' " 2010.

156 "The influenza epidemic did": Gamble, " 'There Wasn't a Lot of Comforts in Those Days,' " 2010.

156 In Philadelphia, some undertakers raised their prices: Crosby, p. 77.

157 The delay in burying the unembalmed dead: "Influenza 1918," *American Experience*, PBS, pbs.org/wgbh/american experience/features/general-article/influenza-philadelphia/.

157   "Wagonloads of bodies, some dead over a week": Armstrong, "Philadelphia, Nurses, and the Spanish Influenza Pandemic of 1918," 2011.

158   "The outside of a face mask is marked": "Sweeping Order Against Influenza in Effect Here Today," *St. Paul Pioneer Press*, November 6, 1918, quoted in Miles Ott et al, "Lessons Learned from the 1918–1919 Influenza Pandemic in Minneapolis and St. Paul, Minnesota," *Public Heath Reports* 122, no. 6 (November–December 2007): p. 803–81, ncbi.nlm.nih.gov/pmc/articles/PMC1997248/.

159   "I personally prefer to take my chances": "Influenza Lid to Go on City Today," *St. Paul Pioneer Press*, November 4, 1918, quoted in Miles Ott et al, "Lessons Learned from the 1918–1919," 2007.

159   "Obey the laws": Billings, "The Public Health Response," 1997.

CHAPTER SEVEN

161   Sick with influenza? Use Ely's Cream Balm: Lynch, "The Flu of 1918," 1998.

162   "No medicine and none of the vaccines": Barry, *The Great Influenza*, pp. 358–359.

162   "Men and women stopped as suddenly as if stabbed": Collier, *The Plague of the Spanish Lady*, p. 57.

163   "The scourge had struck at five continents": Collier, p. 81.

164   "Although he didn't drink himself": Martha Wrigley, "Clarence and Isabelle Ross," War Stories, *Pandemic Influenza Storybook*, April 9, 2013, Centers for Disease Control and Prevention, cdc.gov/publications/panflu/.

165   "My dad came down with the flu": David A. Thompson, "Arne Thompson," War Stories, *Pandemic Influenza Storybook*, April 9, 2013, Centers for Disease Control and Prevention, cdc.gov/publications/panflu/.

166   Frantic shoppers strip pharmacy shelves bare: Lynch, "The Flu of 1918," 1998.

166   "Quacks and naysayers": Julian A Navarro, "Influenza in 1918: An Epidemic in Images," *Public Health Reports* 2010, U.S. National Library of Medicine, ncbi.nlm.nih.gov/pmc/articles/PMC2862330/.

167   "tried everything, everything they could think of": Barry, *The Great Influenza*, p. 358.

168   "Prisoners were thought to be the ideal study subjects": Kolata, *Flu*, p. 57.

169   "maybe those Boston sailors": Kolata, p. 59.

170   "The victims of the epidemic fell on either side": Ernest W. Gibson, "History of the First Vermont and 57th Pioneer Infantry" (address, Montpelier, Vermont, October 23, 1919), quoted in A. Scott Berg, ed., *World War I and America*, pp. 590–592.

171   The conditions during this night: Henry A. May, "The Influenza Epidemic," *History of the U.S.S.* Leviathan (New York, 1919), pp. 160–163, archive.org/details/historyofusslevioobroo.

171   Army hospital authorities removed nearly one thousand: Crosby, *America's Forgotten Pandemic*, pp. 134–135.

172   "Following a week on the front line": Jünger, *Storm of Steel*, p. 263.

172   "Several hundred thousand soldiers": Adam Hochschild, *To End All Wars*, p. 333.

CHAPTER EIGHT

174   "Normally corpses [in India] were cremated": Barry, *The Great Influenza*, p. 365.

175   "The attack was very sudden": Grayson to Tumulty, April 10, 1919.

178   In February 1919: Crosby, *America's Forgotten Pandemic*, p. 176.

178   When Wilson took ill in April: John Milton Cooper Jr., *Woodrow Wilson*, p. 487.

179   "markedly showing the effects": Cooper, p. 488.

179   "The whole of civilization": Cary T. Grayson to Samuel Ross, April 14, 1919, in Michael Alison Chandler, "A President's Illness Kept Under Wraps," *Washington Post*, February 3, 2007, washingtonpost.com/wp-dyn/content/article/2007/02/02/AR2007020201698_2.html.

179   "In half-starving Germany": Hochschild, *To End All Wars*, p. 350.

180 "Cold, hungry, and ragged": Collier, *The Plague of the Spanish Lady*, p. 135.

181 "Prince Max was luckier": Collier, p. 137.

182 More than ten million soldiers died on the battlefields of Europe: Following statistics are cited in Berg, *Wilson*, p. 505.

184 "Ho Chi Minh—and Vietnam": Margaret MacMillan, *Paris 1919*, p. 59.

185 "We shall have to fight": Freedman, *The War to End All Wars*, p. 157.

185 "He was not physically or mentally": Margaret MacMillan, *Paris 1919*, p. 491.

185 The resulting treaty: John Barry, *The Great Influenza*, p. 385.

186 "pathetic, broken Wilson": Margaret MacMillan, *Paris 1919*, p. 182.

186 "In April 1919": Berg, *Wilson*, p. 570.

188 "We could but surmise": Irwin H. Hoover, *Forty-Two Years in the White House* (Boston: Houghton Mifflin, 1934), p. 98, quoted in Barry, *The Great Influenza*, p. 385.

188 "It is of course impossible to say what Wilson would have done": Barry, p. 387.

189 "Health officials realized": Julian A. Navarro, "Influenza in 1918: An Epidemic in Images," *Public Health Reports*, 2010, ncbi.nlm.nih.gov/pmc/articles/PMC2862330/.

190 "Influenza was the likely killer": Hochschild, *To End All Wars*, p. 350.

190 In the Fiji Islands: Barry, p. 364.

190 In March 1919 professional hockey's championship: Adam Gretz, "Remembering when the NHL canceled the Stanley Cup Final due to Flu Pandemic," CBS Sports.com, December 22, 2014, cbssports.com/nhl/news /remembering-when-the-nhl-canceled-the-1919-cup-final-due-to-flu-pandemic/.

191 "The virus burned through the available fuel": Barry, p. 370.

CHAPTER NINE

192 Epidemics create a kind of history from below: Steven Johnson, *The Ghost Map*, p. 32.

194 Hultin later hit on the idea: Kolata, *Flu*, p. 98.

195 "This was a great adventure": Elizabeth Fernandez, "The Virus detective," *SF Gate*, February 17, 2002, sfgate .com/magazine/article/The-Virus-detective-Dr-John-Hultin-has-found-2872017.php.

196 "It took two days to reach the first body": Ned Rozell, "Villager's Remains Lead to 1918 Flu Breakthrough," November 20, 2014, Geophysical Institute, University of Alaska Fairbanks, gi.alaska.edu/alaska-science-forum /villager-s-remains-lead-1918-flu-breakthrough.

196 "In 1951, I was a graduate student": Hultin's account of his time in Brevig in 1951 appears in Kolata, pp. 106–113.

197 "It was like *Raiders of the Lost Ark*": Kolata, p. 204.

197 On this solitary expedition: Elizabeth Fernandez, "The Virus Detective," *SF Gate*, February 17, 2002, sfgate.com /magazine/article/The-Virus-detective-Dr-John-Hultin-has-found-2872017.php.

198 At about the same time: Fernandez, "The Virus Detective," February 17, 2002.

198 "I said that a terrible thing had happened": Kolata, p. 261.

198 Using his wife's pruning shears: Fernandez, "The Virus Detective," February 17, 2002.

200 "For the first time in history": Kolata, p. 307.

200 "When a pathogen": David Quammen, *Spillover*, p. 21.

201 "It is unclear what gave the 1918 virus": Jeffery K. Taubenberger, "The Origin and Virulence of the 1918 'Spanish' Influenza Virus," *Proceedings of the American Philosophical Society* 150, no. 1 (March 2006), p. 90, ncbi.nlm .nih.gov/pmc/articles/PMC2720273/.

201 "Influenza and pneumonia death rates for 15-to-34-year-olds": Taubenberger, "The Origin and Virulence," pp. 90–91.

202   "Essentially people are drowned": "New tests reveal why 1918 flu was so deadly," Associated Press, January 17, 2007, nbcnews.com/id/16670768/ns/health-cold_and_flu/t/new-tests-reveal-why-flu-was-so-deadly/#.WWYq4 MaZNE7.

203   "Never again allow me to say": Quoted in Michael Levin, "An Historical Account of the Influence," *Maryland State Medical Journal* 27, no. 5 (May 1978), p. 61, in Barry, *The Great Influenza*, p. 403.

204   The life expectancy in America: Kolata, *Flu*, p. 7.

208   "Around the world, authorities made plans for international": Barry, p. 398.

AFTERWORD

210   We can only conclude: Jeffery K. Taubenberger and David M. Morens, "1918 Influenza: The Mother of All Pandemics," *Emerging Infectious Diseases* 12, no. 1 (January 2006), pp. 15–22. dx.doi.org/10.3201/eid1201.050979.

212   In 1997, an outbreak of avian: Youngerman, *Pandemics*, p. 322.

213   After a long manhunt: Scott Shane, "FBI, Laying Out Evidence, Closes Anthrax Case," *New York Times*, February 19, 2010, nytimes.com/2010/02/20/us/20anthrax.html.

213   An outbreak of cholera in Haiti: "Haiti Opens Drive to Vaccinate 820,000 as Cholera Flares," *New York Times*, November 9, 2016. nytimes.com/2016/11/10/world/americas/haiti-cholera-hurricane-matthew.html.

213   Chinese authorities were again battling: Chris Buckley, "China Fights Spread of Deadly Avian Virus," *New York Times*, February 18, 2017, nytimes.com/2017/02/18/world/asia/china-bird-flu.html.

214   When the Moline family, turkey farmers in Iowa: Maryn McKenna, "The Looming Threat of Avian Flu," *New York Times Magazine*, April 13, 2016, nytimes.com/2016/04/17/magazine/the-looming-threat-of-avian-flu.html.

214   Since then, Zika has waned almost everywhere: Marina Lopes and Nick Miroff, "The Panic Is Over at Zika's Epicenter, but for Many, the Struggle Has Just Begun," *Washington Post*, February 7, 2017.

215   The unpredictable weather patterns: Maryn McKenna, "Why the Menace of Mosquitoes Will Only Get Worse," *New York Times Magazine*, April 20, 2017, nytimes.com/2017/04/20/magazine/why-the-menace-of-mosquitoes -will-only-get-worse.html.

216   "We can only conclude that since it happened once": Taubenberger and Morens, "1918 Influenza," 2006.

216   "The new vaccine against rotavirus": Donald G. McNeil Jr. "New Vaccine Could Slow Disease That Kills 600 Children a Day," *New York Times*, March 22, 2017, nytimes.com/2017/03/22/health/rotavirus-vaccine.html.

217   "The virus can remain": Barry, *The Great Influenza*, p. 457.

218   "So a terror seeped into the society": Barry, p. 461.

218   "nameless, unreasoning, unjustified terror": Franklin D. Roosevelt, First Inaugural Address, March 4, 1933, as published in Samuel Rosenman, ed., *The Public Papers of Franklin D. Roosevelt, Volume Two: The Year of Crisis, 1933* (New York: Random House, 1938), p. 11–16, on History Matters, historymatters.gmu.edu/d/5057/.

219   "Climate change is turning abnormal weather": McKenna, "Why the Menace of Mosquitoes," April 20, 2017.

219   Tropical diseases "know no borders": Donald G. McNeil Jr., "Trump Plan Eliminates a Global Sentinel Against Disease, Experts Warn," *New York Times*, March 17, 2017, nytimes.com/2017/03/17/health/global-health-fogarty -international-center-viruses.html.

APPENDIX 1

222   The winners of past wars: Diamond, *Guns, Germs, and Steel*, p. 197.

222   For almost two centuries: Kathryn Senior, "How and When Were Bacteria Discovered?" July 6, 2017, Types of Bacteria typesofbacteria.co.uk/how-when-were-bacteria-discovered.html.

225   People in good health: Thucydides, *The History of the Peloponnesian War*, trans. Richard Crawley (New York: E. P. Dutton, 1910), 2.49, in Perseus Digital Library, perseus.tufts.edu/hopper/.

226   Over that time, the plague may have killed a quarter: R. J. Littman, "The Plague of Athens: Epidemiology and Paleopathology," abstract, *Mount Sinai Journal of Medicine* 76, no. 5, (October 2009): pp. 456–67, ncbi.nlm.nih.gov /pubmed/19787658.

226 "Men, not knowing what was to become of them": Thucydides, *Peloponnesian War*, 2.52.

227 They died themselves the most thickly: Thucydides, 2.47.

227 He is also famed for inspiring the phrase: Robert H. Shmerling, "First, Do No Harm," October 13, 2015, *Harvard Health Blog*, health.harvard.edu/blog/first-do-no-harm-201510138421.

228 "Prayer indeed is good": Hippocrates, *Regimen* 4.87, *Hippocrates* vol. 4, trans. W. H. S. Jones (London: William Heinemann, 1959).

228 At that time: Sanjib Khumar Ghosh, "Human cadaveric dissection: a historical account from ancient Greece to the modern era," *Anatomy and Cell Biology*, (September 22, 2015) U.S. National Library of Medicine. ncbi.nlm.nih.gov/pmc/articles/PMC4582158/.

229 "Whatever this pestilence": Lois N. Magner, *A History of Medicine*, p. 74.

230 It is far more likely that an infectious disease: "Intestinal Bug Likely Killed Alexander the Great," news release, June 1, 1998, University of Maryland Medical Center, umm.edu/news-and-events/news-releases/1998/intestinal-bug-likely-killed-alexander-the-great.

234 "as a man might heap up hay in a stack": John of Ephesus, quoted in John Aberth, *Plagues in World History* (London: Rowman & Littlefield, 2011), p. 26.

234 The plague has three different variations: "Plague: Symptoms and Causes," Mayo Clinic, mayoclinic.org/diseases-conditions/plague/symptoms-causes/dxc-20196766.

235 "Every morning, the streets": Magner, p.120.

235 "She ruled in beauty o'er this heart of mine": Petrarch, "Soleasi Nel Mio Cor," VIII, *Fifteen Sonnets of Petrarch*, trans. Thomas Wentworth Higginson (Boston, 1883), sonnets.org/petrarch.htm.

236 "In the year then of our Lord 1348": Giovanni Boccaccio, *The Decameron, or Ten Days Entertainment of Boccaccio*, trans. W. K. Kelley (London, 1872), pp. 29–40, shsu.edu/~his_ncp/Boccaccio.html.

238 Whipping themselves bloody: "The Flagellants Attempt to Repel the Black Death, 1349," EyeWitness to History, 2010, eyewitnesstohistory.com/flagellants.htm.

239 Civilization decreased: Ibn Khaldûn, *The Muqaddimah: An Introduction to History* trans. Franz Rosenthal (Princeton, N.J.: Princeton University Press, 1967), quoted in Youngerman, *Pandemics and Global Health*, p. 198.

244 "As the Indians did not know": Toribio Motolinía, *History of the Indians of New Spain*, ed. and trans. Elizabeth A. Foster (Berkeley: Cortés Society, 1950), p. 8, quoted in Arndt F. Laemmerzahl, "Small Pox," lecture notes, 2008, mason.gmu.edu/~alaemmer/disease/smallpox.pdf.

244 "virgin soil epidemics": Alfred W. Crosby, "Virgin Soil Epidemics as a Factor in the Aboriginal Depopulation in America," *The William and Mary Quarterly* 33, no. 2 (April 1976): pp. 289–299, jstor.org/stable/1922166.

245 "For the natives": John Winthrop to Nathaniel Rich, May 22, 1634, Gilder Lehrman Collection, Gilder Lehrman Institute of American History, gilderlehrman.org.

246 The American Academy of Pediatrics: "Ipecac," A Minute for Kids, American Academy of Pediatrics, aap.org.

246 Inoculation, or variolation, had been used: Elizabeth A. Fenn, *Pox Americana*, p. 31.

246 The idea had come from a slave: David McCullough, *John Adams* (New York: Simon & Schuster, 2001), p. 142.

246 A prominent Puritan minster: Fenn, p. 41.

248 "With the exception of the war itself": Fenn, p. 9.

254 "For almost two centuries, the knowledge": Senior, "How and When Were Bacteria Discovered?" July 6, 2017.

255 she was quarantined: Filio Marineli, Gregory Tsoucalas, Marianna Karamanou, and George Androutsos, "Mary Mallon (1869–1938) and the history of typhoid fever," Annals of Gastroenterology 2013, ncbi.nlm.nih.gov/pmc/articles/PMC3959940/.

256 "screaming and cursing them": Deborah Blum, *The Poisoner's Handbook*, p. 5.

257 "With the growing and profound knowledge": Kolata, *Flu*, p. 47.

260   July 1916: "Whatever Happened to Polio?" Communities, *The American Epidemics*, Smithsonian National Museum of American History, amhistory.si.edu/polio/americanepi/communities.htm.

263   One was in South Sudan: "Ebola Virus Disease," fact sheet, June 2017, World Health Organization, who.int /mediacentre/factsheets/fs103/en/.

APPENDIX 2

264   The Centers for Disease Control and Prevention: "CDC Says 'Take 3' Actions to Fight the Flu," August 1, 2016, cdc.gov/flu/protect/preventing.htm.

ACKNOWLEDGMENTS

THIS BOOK GREW out of a chance conversation near the elevators in my publisher's office as I commiserated with a flu-stricken editor. When she mentioned her interest in a book on the Spanish Flu, in part because of the loss of a family member to the pandemic, the idea for a book took hold. So my first thanks go to editor Sally Doherty for helping to send me on this incredible journey to uncover the largely forgotten story of the Spanish Flu and its connection to the events in the final months of World War I. In addition to the inspiration, she once again proved to be an insightful and rigorous editor, and I am grateful for her contribution to this book.

I am also especially indebted to managing editor Jennifer Healey for her careful reading and editing of the manuscript. I have learned a great deal from her and I am grateful for her exacting devotion to accuracy.

The entire team at Henry Holt Books for Young Readers has again provided wonderful support. I am deeply appreciative for the dedicated assistance, enthusiasm, and talents of Christian Trimmer, Rachel Murray, Patrick Collins, Johanna Kirby, Allison Verost, Katie Halata, Kelsey Marrujo, Molly Brouillette Ellis, Tom Nau, Melissa Croce, Lucy Del Priore, and Jessica Anderson.

As always, I am ever grateful for the support of my family. As a Family Nurse Practitioner and student of history, Jenny Davis made extremely valuable contributions to this book. Colin Davis also offered his insights and encouragement. My wife, Joann Davis, has always been my greatest support and most demanding reader. Her wisdom and guidance have made my work possible.

INDEX